A
DROP
OF
Grace

Dennis Page

Contents

Dedication

*This book is gratefully
dedicated to:*

*J*esus Christ, the Lamb of God, for redeeming my life from destruction and crowning me with loving kindness and tender mercy. For His great sacrifice, the blood He shed that paid the penalty for my sins. For revealing Himself to me at a time in my life when I thought it was about to end. For showing me an example of how I am to live a Christian life through the grace that He freely gives, and His continued intercession on my behalf.

God the Father, for giving His only Son to redeem us from the snares of Satan, a gift of love that will be spoken of for all eternity. I will praise my heavenly Father in the midst of the congregation, will go where You would have me go and say what You would have me to say. It is my joy to bring honor to your Name.

Acknowledgements

With loving acknowledgements:

To my lovely wife, Melody, who has assisted me with developing my testimony. For her prayers and encouragement, for being so patient with me in trying times, her sacrifices and willingness to endure hardship for the spreading of the gospel. May our God enrich your life with deeper manifestations of His love.

To my son, Travis, who has loved me regardless of my past, and has encouraged me in trying times. I thank him for his patience and sharing me with others that they too may come to know Jesus Christ. Thank you, my son, for your love, compassion, and being supportive of the ministry the Lord has called me to. May God manifest Himself to you in an even greater way than He has me.

To my brothers and sisters in Christ Jesus who ministered to me out of their Bible school when I was in prison, sending me Bible studies, books and lifting me up in prayer. May God richly bless their ministry.

Introduction

"He also brought me up out of a horrible pit, out of the miry clay, and set my feet upon a rock, and established my steps." Psalm 40:2

One dark and weary night, when all odds seemed to be stacked against me, and when hopelessness and despair filled my heart, God sent an angel to open my eyes to the One who loves abundantly and seeks to save those that are lost. When all I embraced was darkness, light came, and with it, peace. As I reflected on my life, I found myself overwhelmed with fear and anxiety. However, I believed there was more to this visit than just the message given. This inspired me to pick up a Bible and search to know God.

It is my hope that in telling my life's story, you will find that the same peace and love that I found in Christ can be a part of your life as well. Whatever may have been your past experiences, and however discouraging your present circumstances may be, if you will come to Jesus just as you are—weak, helpless, and despairing—our compassionate Savior is waiting and watching to embrace you upon your cry for help. He tells us, *"The one who comes to Me I will by no means cast out"* (John 6:37). He is truly the only One who can set us free from sin, heal our broken hearts, and transform our feeble minds. His invitation continues to sound to all today, *"Come to Me, all you who labor and are heavy laden, and I will give you rest"* (Matthew 11:28).

It is the darkness of misconception of God that is enshrouding the world. Men are losing the knowledge of His character and grace. However, the last rays of merciful light, and the last message of mercy to be given to this dying world, will be a revelation of His character of love.

I invite you to read my story with your Bible in hand that you may look up the verses that I make reference to, that you may hear the voice of God to your soul, that your joy may be full. May you be inspired, encouraged, and challenged by the testimony of my life and experiences with Jesus Christ.

Chapter 1

Growing Up

"Thou tellest my wonderings: put thou my tears into Thy bottle: are they not in Thy book?" Psalm 56:8, KJV

I was born in Buffalo, New York, and my parents named me Dennis Earl Smith, after my father. There is not much I know about my father, except his name and that at one time he served in the U.S. Navy on an aircraft carrier. I was still an infant when my mother became pregnant with my sister. Perhaps the quick growth of the family was too much stress, or there were other troubles in their young marriage, but shortly after her birth, my parents separated.

When I was seven, my mother remarried. I remember that day clearly because of something my mother said to me. I had been looking through what I remember to be a children's Bible at my grandmother's house when she said that God is going to destroy the world in the year 2000 by fire. I don't know what made her say this but I was shocked to hear this, of course. I could not understand why God would do such a thing. I remembered grabbing a pen and paper to try to figure out how old I would be when I would die due to this destruction. I would be 37 years old. Needless to say, this did not give me a very good picture of the character of God. Why would He show up only to just burn us up?

What kind of God is He? In the meantime, I put these questions at the back of my mind, the year 2000 seemed a very long way off then, but the thought would come back to me from time to time as I was growing up. Shortly after this my mother gave birth to my younger brother, my sister and I would help take care of him.

I did not grow up in a Christian home. My stepfather grew up in a Methodist family while my mom was raised Catholic, but neither my mother nor my stepfather practiced their religion or attended church. I had only been to church a few times with my grandparents when I was young and don't recall much of it. Growing up, our parents told us not to do this and that, to be polite and not to steal—kind of a basic outline on how to be good. We were told to *"Do as I say and not as I do."* Well, of course, this raised many questions in my young mind, like, *"Why can they do some things and we can't? Why do parents say that it is wrong to do something, and yet they do it?"* I think it was at this time the seed of rebellion was planted in my heart. I thought then that when I got older I would do what I wanted, just like my parents. At the age of ten my mother gave me my first drink thinking that it would discourage me from drinking. By the time I was thirteen my stepfather taught me how to gamble and round this time I came across some pornographic materials he left lying around, and this perverted my mind in the way I looked at a woman.

From a very young age up through my teenage years, I was shy and kept to myself most of the time. I seemed to be small for my age and was made fun of often. Growing up, deep in my heart, I was searching for love and affection; for purpose and meaning. Later on the friends I made came from different backgrounds; however, we all had one thing in common and that was we all had little adult supervision in our life. None of our parents ever seemed to be in the picture. I wanted to fit in, so I started to drink and do drugs with the rest of the kids. I just wanted to be loved and accepted. Many times I was disciplined for wrong doing but after becoming calloused to the stern hand placed upon me, I began to rebel more.

I spent most of my time watching TV, building models, playing games, and running around the neighborhood with friends, causing mischief. At times I was not very respectful to our elderly neighbors. To me they seemed to be very crabby and not very kind to young people. My friends and I would play street football after school. They would sometimes watch us kids play football, and as soon as the ball went on their grass they would try to beat us to it and keep it, yelling at us for walking on their grass. There was one particular neighbor who had a wrought iron fence that enclosed his front yard. When the ball went in his yard he would smile, come down off the porch, then take the ball and go inside his house. I thought to myself how mean it was for him to do that.

But I also really liked school and enjoyed seeing the look on Mom's face when I brought home a report card with all A's. I got my first job as a paperboy at the age of twelve. My parents did not have a lot of money, and we did not own a car until I was fourteen. I did not want to be poor like that when I grew up so I took my mother's advice to work hard and to be on time. They also taught me how to be responsible by requiring a portion of my income to help with the family's bills. I loved my parents, but we did not have much family time together. After coming home from work, my mom would make dinner while my stepfather watched his favorite TV programs. My siblings and I would eat dinner in the kitchen while they ate in the living room, watching TV. We could only join them after we finished all our food and did the dishes.

As the years went by, TV and video games became an escape from reality for me. I, like most children, was greatly stimulated by the funny cartoons that showed aggression, immorality, and magic which promotes witchcraft. All these primed my mind for more suspense, drama, and action-packed movies. The more suspense and violence in the movies the more intrigued I was. It was even better when video games came along; they were not as intense as they are today, but it was captivating to my mind. These things absorbed my attention, and I could not wait to watch my favorite program or play my games. I would also find myself replaying the video game repeatedly in my mind. I would often lay awake at night thinking of how I could live my life like those actors I had seen in the movies. Although I often wondered what it would be like to be the hero, I just did not see myself ever being one. Also, the hero was not much different from the bad guys. He smokes, drinks, uses foul language, destroys things, uses witchcraft, murders the bad guy, and often commits fornication with the woman in distress. The more I watched, the more I was drawn to the lifestyle of the villain. It seemed they were the ones really living the life. They had all the excitement and fun, and they were respected and feared. It looked like they had the power, money, respect and no boundaries. And although in the movies the villains may die or go to prison, I would just make up my own ending because I thought that if I could live like that I would do something different and not get caught. Little did I realize that I was slowly but surely being molded by all these things.

I realized now that many parents raise their children with only the knowledge that was passed down to them by their own parents. If they grew up in a dysfunctional, unloving, or abusive family, often these same abuses and habits are passed down to the next generation. But many parents fail to realize that their behavior and the things they partake of have a great influence on their children. They set the stage, to large degree, for their children's character development and what a child sees and hears leaves deep impressions on their young minds that are hard to efface.

When I was fourteen, my parents decided to move to a small town in Indiana. I was finishing eighth grade and was not at all interested in changing schools or meeting new kids. After the move, I pretty much kept to myself during the remainder of the school year. I was bored because they were teaching what I had already been taught in the sixth grade. I could not figure out why they were so far behind. On the other hand, it was neat because I did not have to do any studying for about two years.

During my high school years, the few friends I did have would drink, get high, and run the streets all in the name of fun. Like most teenagers, again, I just wanted to fit in so I went along with the crowd. On my sophomore year, a group of us were out drinking one night. We were driving through this neighborhood when we suddenly stopped in front of one of the houses and everyone got out of the car, including myself. Someone in the group had been doing home invasions. At first I did not know what was happening, but then a friend told me what our other friend was up to, and we all in our drunken stupor, just went along. We entered the house and just took things at random, then piled into our cars and left. I thought that was fun, not giving much thought on the possibility of getting caught. This led to another and yet still another home invasion.

The day of reckoning finally came; I was finally brought in for questioning. The kid that had led out that first night had been a part of another group that had robbed several homes. He was finally caught, and to save his own hide, he turned in everyone he knew. We were all convicted and sentenced to jail time, probation, and had to make restitution. I was only fifteen, and already sitting in a jail cell, alone and ashamed of what I had done. After seven days my parents came to picked me up. I told them on the way home that I was sorry and had learned my lesson. I assured them I would never do that again. But my promises were like ropes of sand as I continue to hang around the same people, I was soon drawn back to doing things I promised not to do. Like so many others, I never planned on becoming an alcoholic, drug user and theft as a teenager but through association I became changed.

Because of my unruly behavior, my stepfather would often threaten to send me to some type of military school for obedience train-ing. At the age of sixteen, near the end of my junior year, I figured I would beat him to it. I spoke with a Marine Corps recruiter to see what it would take for me to join the Marines. He told me that if my parents would sign a waiver, I could start going to reserve meetings during my senior year, and after my graduation I could go to boot camp. I de-cided to do this. I wanted to prove to my parents that I had no problem with discipline, but that my problem was in trying to understand their example of, *"Don't do as I do, but do as I say."* When the recruiter came to the house, my parents happily signed the papers and so, with their approval, I began reserve meetings and after graduation I was off. I completed my boot camp training and then trained to be a combat engineer. It was severe and intense, but I made it through and finished in the top ten percent of my unit, earning a stripe. I returned home, attended reserve meetings, and started a full-time job.

During these years, I had no idea that the great Creator of the universe was taking note of my life. He was taking note of how I was being influenced by the people and circumstances that surrounds me, extending His longsuffering towards me as He waited for me to answer His call. He was collecting every tear that I shed because of childhood discouragements, disappointments, and broken relationships as a young man. He also recorded in a book His appeals to my heart to come to Him, my convictions and my responses (See Daniel 7:10; Revelation 20:11-15.)

Chapter 2

Filling the Void

"Vanity of vanities, all is vanity." Ecclesiastes 1: 2

After returning home from the Marines, I was looking forward to getting my own place. However, to my surprise, the money that I had sent home for savings was gone. My parents told me that they had to use the money to pay restitution for a robbery I had been accused of. I was hanging out with a friend one night, and he asked me to help him pick up the last of his things from his old apartment. Well, I was not aware that in the process of getting his things he helped himself to some of his roommates' items. I tasted the bitter consequences of being with the wrong person at the wrong time. A wise man once said, "The righteous should choose his friends carefully, for the way of the wicked leads them astray" (Proverbs 12:26). Although I was never brought up on any charges, my parents believed the person who accused me and paid him some of that money. I also knew my stepfather's addiction to gambling, which probably explained where the rest of the money had gone.

It did not take me long to I realized that there still seemed to be a void in my life. Although I thought being a marine would bring me respect and a sense of purpose, I was mistaken. I was eighteen, and my heart was still searching for love and a sense of belonging. I got a full-time job, did reserve meetings during the month, and went back to using drugs. I started using and selling cocaine along with other drugs to cover my costs. I liked to party, but I was against using my paycheck for it. It was here I began to experience what I thought was respect and acceptance. The void in my heart seemed to disappear as more people came to me and desired to be around me. I did not see anything wrong with what I was doing. I was comparing myself to those around me. Besides, I was just supplying a demand. I reasoned to myself that if people don't get it from me they would just get it from somebody else. In my mind there was not much difference between those addicted to caffeine, liquor, and nicotine and those who used weed and cocaine or other drugs. After all, a drug is a drug whether it is legal or not.

As I continued to keep up with this lifestyle, pride grew and so did my addiction. The void in my heart would return from time to time and I would fill it with a new drug, a different woman, and more material things. Over the next twenty years failed relationships, and the loss of friends due to addiction would become the norm of my life. During one relationship I had, all she wanted was for me to stop using and selling cocaine. She would tell me that it was becoming a greater problem now than when we first met, and that if I loved her I would quit. Well, I struggled with this. You see, my concept of love was that I was providing a place for her to stay, clothing, food, and bought her nice things, so therefore I must love her. So what is her problem? I thought this was how you were supposed to show someone that you loved them. This is what I learned, and so this is all I knew. I had a good job, a nice place to stay, many material things, and I paid my bills. There was no way in the world she could convince me that I had a drug problem or that I did not love her. It was here that I deceived myself, and it is here that most people with addictions do as well. I thought everyone else had the problem, not me. Addicts will very rarely see their lives as unmanageable or out of control.

Then one day during an argument, I just packed up a few items, got in my car and left. I never tried to reconcile and just went on my way, doing what I wanted to do with the same attitude that nobody was going to tell me how to live my life. The result was a lifestyle of selfishness, doing what I want to do regardless of the effect it had on those around me. I was drawn to the power of having something that people needed due to their addiction, the sense of purpose I was experiencing, the way I felt being the center of attention, and the fear or respect I received. These things only increased the selfishness and pride in my heart.

Within a few months, I started dating again, a relationship started for all the wrong reasons. We both liked to party and nice things. I was searching for someone that would not care about my lifestyle. I was looking for a party partner. When I was thirty, she gave birth to my son. Although I loved him and enjoyed watching him grow, it did not change things for me as a drug dealer and user. Once again, because of this, our relationship fell apart and within four years, we went our separate ways. I would keep my son with me three or four days a week and she would keep him the other half. I thanked God that she realized it was best for him to be involved in my life. He was the one thing that kept me somewhat accountable for my behavior. But it would take many more years for me to understand and see that building a relationship based on money, sex, drugs, and other selfish reasons would always result in emptiness and heartache.

My friend, if you are looking for a lifelong mate, I encourage you to seek God's guidance. Respect God-given boundaries and not to be unequally yoked. To enter into a relationship expecting to bring the other person up to speed or to convert them could be disastrous. Put God first. Don't be afraid to let Him choose for you. Now you may be thinking that He does not know what you need. That's where we make a big mistake. Only God can see the heart of an individual and know that person's capabilities. God will match you with the person who will be a blessing to you; perhaps one who will help you see yourself as you really are while revealing to you through their love a deeper revelation of God's love. Yes, God understand that there needs to be physical attraction too but we should be more concerned about the condition of the person's heart than how good looking they are otherwise you may end up with a beautiful person on the outside but is not on the inside.

But up until I've given my life to the Lord, I really did not care about anything or anyone else but myself. I was never able to see how my life was affecting those around me because I was too busy chasing the "rush" or "high" from the things I was doing. The street term for this is *"chasing the dragon"* and how fitting this is to describe the life I was living as I continued to chase after things to satisfy pride, and perverted pleasures. Yes, chasing the dragon—Satan, for these are his characteristics (See Revelation 12:9.)

Chapter 3

An Invitation

*"Come unto Me, all you who labor and are heavy laden,
and I will give you rest." Matthew 11:28*

At the age of thirty-five my employer, at that time, invited me to go to church with him. His invitation caught me off guard. You see, he knew that I used and sold drugs, but that did not bother him. I was a good worker, and that is all most employers care about, but this man and his wife were different. God was reaching out to me, but I did not understand. My employer and his wife showed me kindness, and I believe really cared about my salvation. However, I refused their invitation. You see, I believed that my fate was sealed because of the things that I have done and was still doing. I heard of a place called heaven and hell and because of the choices I had made, hell was the place for me and there was nothing I could do about it. Then he asked if they could take my son to church. This I agreed to and I don't know where this thought came from but it just came out. I told him that if I was ever going to do anything right with my life, I wanted my son to know who Jesus is. You see, I have heard the name of Jesus before but I knew nothing about Him. Nevertheless, I believed there was hope for my son, who was only six years old at that time. I thought that if he could know Jesus he would have a better chance than I did. For myself, I thought there was no hope. They happily took my son to church a couple of times, and he really enjoyed himself. God was seeking to draw me to Him through my son, but I was too entangled with darkness to see or understand this. Someday I hope to thank this couple for their kindness and prayers.

Shortly after this, a coworker invited me and my son to go to church with his family and this time I decided to go. I went to church with him and his wife about three or four times, but for the wrong reasons. I was tired of the type of women I was meeting, and I thought it might be nice to meet a Christian woman. And so instead of listening to what the preacher was saying and following along in the Bible, I was too busy checking out the ladies. However, it was not long before I started to feel like a hypocrite. I thought to myself, *what are you doing here? You will just corrupt these people.* Although my son enjoyed himself, after a few times I stopped going; I just did not feel right going to church then going home, getting high, and making a deal. I just could not see this part of my life changing. I was just evil, and I did not see any hope for a person like me.

I did realize later in life that we are not to base our relationship with Jesus upon feelings. Although I did not feel right going to church, singing praise songs, and listening to the Word because of the things I was doing in life, I really should have kept going. I thought I needed to be a good person first before I could ever go to church or read His Word. I had it all backwards. To think like this would be like taking a bath first so that you can take a shower later. It is impossible for us to clean ourselves up before we go to Jesus. I did not understand then that I could come to Him with all my dirt and baggage of life, and if I would ask for pardon He would grant it. In Isaiah 1:18, God invites us to come and reason with Him, and that He is more than able to clean us up. Jesus is in the business of saving people, not condemning them (See John 3:17.) He has promised that whoever comes to Him He would not turn away (See John 6:37 emphasis mine.)

Chapter 4

Deeper into the Quicksand

"The way of the wicked is like darkness:
They do not know what makes them stumble." Proverbs 4:19

O ver the next couple of years, I started dealing drugs heavily. I switched from cocaine to meth. I was burnt out on cocaine after seventeen years of use, and I started smoking and selling meth because it was becoming a very popular drug. From time to time I would rent out one of the extra bedrooms in my house in order to help pay the bills. One time I rented to one of the people whom I was buying from, I'll call him *Sergio*. I started to meet some of his friends, and occasionally I would see the person he picked up from. I'll call him *John*.

After a while, things were not going too well. I was in need of product, and Sergio would just hold out. I knew he had it, and I did not understand what his problem was. I had established a steady flow of business, and I did not want to lose my customers to another supplier. So one time when John called for Sergio, I answered the phone, I told him that Sergio was not around and then I asked if I could meet with him and talk about some things. He agreed, and we met the next day.

*Names have been changed

I then started doing business directly with John. A short time later I asked Sergio to move out so there would not be any contention between us. But I was always looking for an opportunity to move up the ladder or establish a better business relationship with the organization. Pride and selfishness fed the hunger for power and position. I've always thought of self and did not care to think or contemplate the consequences of my actions.

I was, at this time of my life, hungry for more of power and position that nothing else seem to matter, not even somebody else's life. This became apparent to me one day when not long after Sergio moved out of my place a man came to my house to do business with me. It turned out that this man was in trouble with Sergio and John. I turned him in so they could do away with him. And this happened again at another occasion where I've given information that may have caused this man his life. I never thought that I would reach a point so low that self is all I cared about, to get and gain at the expense of another human life!

Never kid yourself when it comes to using and dealing drugs, you will do things that you never thought you would do. How selfishness and pride consumed me to the point that I was willing to destroy another human life. ***Oh, how far I had sunk in the quicksand of sin!*** I could not see how I was a slave to Satan and could only do his bidding.

Not long after this, I discovered what I believed to be the true identity of a couple of people working undercover within the organization. I knew this would be valuable information to John and others. With evidence in hand, I set up a meeting with John the next day. As I shared these things with John, he was struggling to believe this because he had known these individuals for quite some time. However, as I presented to him evidences, he became concerned. He then set up a meeting a couple days later so that I could share this information with someone higher up in the organization. With this new information I thought it would be best if I took some extra precautions and picked up some tracking devices that would tell me if I was under surveillance. It was not long after this that I discovered my phone was tapped and that the task force had set up a surveillance team around my home. With the new technology and having been in the game for so long, I was always one step ahead of them, or so I thought.

A short time later I was having lunch with John at a restaurant that belonged to his friend. We sat at a table at the back of the restaurant. During lunch, he excused himself, saying that he had to go outside to talk to someone. Soon after he left, a man came walking in with his hands in his jacket pockets. Now this was out of the ordinary, as he was wearing a heavy jacket in the middle of summer. This put me on the alert, but I thought there were too many people around for something to go down, so I remained calm. As he approached, I noticed he was looking around the room to see if anybody was watching our table. He stopped next to my table, turned, and looked around the room again, then sat down in the chair right across from me. He continued to watch the people. However, he never looked directly at me, and he kept his hands in his pockets the whole time. I just kept eating my lunch. After a few more minutes, he got up and left. Then John came back in and we finished our lunch. I did not ask him what was going on, I just figured this was the organization's way of testing me.

A couple days later, I got a call from John; he wanted to stop by to pick up some money. When I opened the door to let him in, I noticed that the man sitting in the car was the same one that walked into the restaurant a couple of days before. I confronted John and asked him what was going on. He assured me all was well and there was no need for alarm. I was not stupid; after dealing with these people, I knew that if they were unsure of what to believe regarding the information I had presented to them the organization would just eliminate all of us to protect themselves. In this type of business you are just a dollar sign, and if it appears that you can't be trusted or you pose a threat, they deal with it as they see fit to protect themselves. This became even clearer to me one day when a hit man from another organization came to my house looking for Sergio. Apparently, he owed them a lot of money and he was not paying. Perhaps they also suspected something was up. The price on his head was just three thousand dollars. How little a human life is valued! Still it did not bother me; I just looked at the whole situation as if I was in some action-packed movie, as if I was just an "actor" playing a part.

Over the next few months things became even more intense around me and in the organization. I was in too deep to walk away and, sad to say, I just never valued my own life that much. My thoughts were if there was no excitement in your life, you were not living. However, I never realized just how deep I had sunk in darkness, stumbling down the path to destruction.

Today, as I consider my past, I am humbled by the depth of God's mercy and the breath of His love. How many times He had intervened to spare my life and every time I had made decisions that would directly cost another person their life, in the days and years ahead, I would discover that God intervened to deliver that person also. This I would discover first hand. For a couple years I would keep running into my old friend, *Frank*, during these prison ministry visits. I asked God why I kept running into him. I was then impressed that I needed to apologize for the decisions I've made that could have cost him his life. So, next time I saw Frank, I asked him to come to the front with me. I gave a little background on how I knew him, and in front of other inmates, I asked for his forgiveness. I shared how I bought in the lies of Satan and became his slave for many years. I encouraged him and other inmates to decide to be no longer a slave to him anymore.

I was completely self-deceived, I was doing things I thought I would never do because all that mattered was pleasing self. After all, how could I value another human life when I had no respect for my own? Later when I came to the cross for the first time, I would see just a glimpse of the value our heavenly Father placed upon me by giving up His only begotten Son to pay the price for my sins. "Yet I will not forget you. See, I have inscribed you on the palms of My hands" (Isaiah 49:16). Don't trust your feelings friend, just look to the cross on Calvary. It is here that every human being will see that they are of infinite value to the Creator of mankind. For God so loved you and me that He gave His only begotten Son that if we would believe on Him we would not perish but have everlasting life (See John 3:16.)

Chapter 5

Talking with Spirits

"There shall not be found among you...one who practices witchcraft, or a soothsayer, or one who interprets omens, or a sorcerer, or one who conjures spells or a medium, or a spiritist, or one who calls up the dead."
Deuteronomy 18:10, 11

long with the drug abuse going on in my life, a friend introduced me to talking with the spirits. This particular friend called me up one evening and asked if I would visit her where she was house sitting, When I got there we partied for a little bit and then she started sharing with me how she had been talking with spirits since she was a child. These spirits of dead people, she believed, would give her information or messages from time to time. These all sounded new and intriguing to me. *It seems the dead are not really dead,* I thought to myself. So, I stood there fascinated and as we continued talking an expression came over her face like she was going in a trance. She then said one of the spirits would like to communicate with me and started to describe the spirit. The description she gave exactly fit that of my grandmother who had died many years ago. I have never talked about my grandmother to my friend or has she seen a picture of her before. Needless to say, I was amazed and impressed by this (as this was the purpose) and waited for more. I truly believed it was the spirit of my grandmother. My friend then said the message from my grandmother was that I should spend more time with my son. This really got my attention because I was so caught up with the drug game and I was slacking off as a father. I didn't really understand what has happening that night but this would impact my life later on.

A couple of days went by and strange things started happening around my house. Things will turn on and off by themselves and there were many times I would feel a "presence" around me. At one point while I was visiting again with this friend, she told me that these spirits would like to communicate directly to me and show me things. At first I was a little scared but as time went on I grew accustomed to what's taking place around me. It was at this time that they started revealing things that appeared to be of great benefit to me. Plots and schemes against me I was now being made aware of. I thought then that I had tapped into the ultimate source of power. This only fed my pride, thinking I was untouchable my desire for power over others grew even more. Later on, however, I discovered that when I decided to turn to God and call on Him for help, these same spirits turned against me in a very vicious way, which I remember distinctly to this day. Up until that time I did not know that we are not supposed to have anything to do with spirits or people that claimed to talk with the dead. All this would become clear to me after I started to study the Bible.

I, like many others, was fascinated with the afterlife. I see more movies each year coming out claiming that we are able to and there is nothing wrong with communicating with the dead. More and more people claim to be psychics, that they have the gift of "crossing over", of being able to predict and see things to come, to warn their loved ones. All of these I would later discover that God strictly forbids such practices for very good reasons. As I would learn from the Bible that these are spirits of devils working miracles and deceiving all that do not know the Word of God (See 2 Corinthians 11:13-15; Revelation 13:14; 16:14.)

For more information about this topic, check out the free Bible study offer by Amazing Facts on page 173 for topics such as *"Are the Dead Really Dead?"* and *"Is the Devil in charge of Hell."*

Chapter 6

A Close Call

"The Lord… is longsuffering toward us, not willing that any should perish but that all should come to repentance." 2 Peter 3:9

One night while sitting at home, I got a phone call from a very angry man. His ex-girlfriend had been buying from me, and he did not like it. I responded the only way I knew how and told him to come over, that I had something for him. Meanwhile, I had to shovel some snow off my roof. There was quite a bit of snow, and the ice was backing up under my shingles, causing water to leak into the house. I thought I would go up to do that and at the same time check out what the surveillance team might be up to. By now I had pretty much figured out which vehicles they were using. I also thought I should take a weapon out with me in case the caller stop by.

I took a 9 mm rifle and my scanner with me so I could listen to what the police were doing. As soon as I walked out front and turned to lock my door, I heard a report came over the scanner: *"Subject has a weapon."* I looked around, but I thought I was just being paranoid. *They can't be talking about me.* Then, as I was walking toward the back of the house, I heard them say, *"Subject is going around back."* Then I knew! A few days earlier I thought I had seen a couple of officers in my neighbor's house across the street, but I was not sure. They had their blinds pulled down, and all I could see was the lower part of some uniforms. They had a big bay window in the front of their house, and never in the six years I had been living there had they ever shut the blinds. Now I knew the police had set up across the street.

I proceeded around back and up the ladder; I got up on the roof and just stood there for a couple of minutes, listening for what they might say next. I started to shovel snow off the roof when I heard, *"Dispatch, this is squad two requesting permission to pull out. Subject is on the roof with weapon."* I stopped shoveling and for a moment just watched. I could see the neighborhood pretty well from my roof. An SUV came around from the street behind my house; two snowmobiles and a van came from down the street. They all met behind some woods just down the street across from the front of my house. I just stared, listening for their next move. Then it came over the scanner: *"Dispatch, squad two requesting permission to jump the gun."* I knew then it was not going to be good! They were requesting to come over and take me out! I suppose they thought I was going to use my firearm to engage them in a conflict.

I did not hesitate. I left the rifle on the roof, went into the house and called my mother. I know you might be thinking, *I thought you were a tough guy!* Yes, I called my mother; I have always been open with my mother about what I was doing. She did not like it, but I was her son, and she still loved me and always hoped I would walk away from that lifestyle. I knew my phone was tapped, so I figured that if I repeated the reason why I had the weapon in the first place, they might get the message.

After the conversation with my mom, I went back up on the roof to watch for their next move. Within minutes, the answer came over the scanner. *"Squad two, this is dispatch. That is a negative on 'jump the gun,' subject has weapon for trespasser only."* I watched as they slowly drove off. I finished shoveling off the roof and went inside. God had saved my life again, and I did not even know it was Him that intervened. His goodness was passing before me and His mercy was abundant, but I was still too blind and proud to see it.

Today, when I reflect on my past I can see the many times God was seeking to woo me to Him by the multitude of mercies that He showed to me. I am not able to count all the times that I should have died from drug overdose or should have been killed due to the things

I was doing. The love of God for fallen humanity is so deep. So the Word of God is fulfilled and His character is revealed. "The Lord, the Lord God, merciful and gracious, longsuffering, and abounding in goodness and truth, keeping mercy for thousands, forgiving iniquity and transgression and sin.... Not willing that any should perish but that all should come to repentance." (See Exodus 34:6, 7; 2 Peter 3:9.)

Chapter 7

Touched by an Angel

"For thus says the Lord God; Indeed I Myself will search for My sheep and seek them out. I will seek what was lost and bring back what was driven away, bind up the broken and strengthen what was sick." Ezekiel 34:11, 16

A couple of weeks passed and I was really getting tired of my lifestyle, and I knew it was just a matter of time before I would end up dying either from too much dope, or one of the two groups would kill me. But what could I do? I was in too deep and I did not know how to get out. For several months I would write out my feelings, but many times I would just cry from loneliness. I had a very nice home with everything in it. I had an in-ground pool, nice car, and money did not seem to be a problem. I had respect from those around me and had many friends. Just what I thought life was all about. However, I still felt so empty inside.

It was after another big party at my house when I reached the lowest point in my life. Everyone had left; I just sat there and began to reflect back on my life. First, I became angry with my parents for the way they raised me, as all I could see was their shortcomings. Then, I was heartbroken over failed relationships and was tired of the current ones, knowing these women were just there for the party, as were most of my so-called friends. At the back of my mind I wondered, *is this all there is to life, to work and party, then grow old and die?* I was overwhelmed by these thoughts. What was I missing? I did not understand. The pain inside was too much. I finally reached the point where I did not care if I live or die. At about 2:00 a.m. I got out a pen and pad and started to write again to try to express the pain I was feeling inside. I started writing, but this time, for some unexplained reason, I started out with the words "Jesus said." I did not know Jesus, let alone what He said. I had never read the Bible before, but the words flowed out, so I titled it

"As Words Flow through Me to You":

Jesus said, for I told you, I would never be far away as I feel and hear your hearts cry out today.
The people said, what must we do? Where should we pray?
And where is it safe for our children to play?
With all the evil in the world today, our Savior, can you say?
Jesus said, the answers have been placed in your hearts from the very start. True faith will see you through.
The people said, with all the evil in the world today, is it our faith we are to rely on?
Jesus said, yes, for the end days have now come. I will test the faith in everyone.
I said, Have no fear for Jesus is here. Do you not feel Him?
Is it not clear? His Spirit is everywhere. Put all your trust and faith in the Father and the Son, and they will guide you and protect you from the wicked one. I also would like people to live their lives with this in mind.
Treat the person next to you as if that person was Jesus Christ, and then, and only then, will the world be a better place for you, and me, and our families.

After I finished writing these words, I put the paper aside and began to write something else. All of a sudden, I heard loud footsteps running down my hallway upstairs. This caused my heart to jump. I was aware of the spirit activity going on around my house, but I had never heard one make so much noise. With my heart racing, I went back to writing. Then from out of the corner of my eye I caught a glimpse of a silhouette of a person standing on the right side of the room; it was there for a moment then gone. For some reason this presence did not scare me, but a sense of peace came over me and I continued to write. And as I did so the figure again appeared and then walked over to where I was and sat down beside me. I wanted to look but I could not. It was as if my head was locked in place. Then I heard a voice say, *"Keep writing,"* so I did. When I was done, I picked up the first paper and began to read it. Peace and hope began to fill my heart as I read. It was as if God had placed His arms around me, and for the first time in my life I felt the comforting love and presence of God. I was then able to look to my side where the figure was, but the messenger was gone. Overwhelmed with joy, I began to dance around the room kind of foolishly. I knew then that Jesus is real.

Today, there is no doubt in my mind the Lord sent an angel to encourage me in the darkest time of my life, to reveal to me that God loved me and wanted to set me free from sin. I would come to understand that God was not condemning me nor counting my sin against me, but with longing desire He wanted to reconcile me to Himself through Jesus Christ. Later I would read, "Can a woman forget her nursing child, and not have compassion on the son of her womb? Surely, they may forget, yet I will not forget you. See, I have inscribed you upon the palms of My hands" (Isaiah 49:16, 17).

Our families and friends may cast us off, but Jesus and His Father would never forget us. We are forever engraved upon Jesus' hands through the crucifixion. God our Father promised that through His Son, Jesus Christ, He would seek out that which was lost, bring back those that have been driven away, would bind up the broken hearted and strengthen those that have been sick. Little did I know the journey Jesus was about to take me on to demonstrate the power of His grace. Several months later, as I read the Bible, the following passages and more affected my life. Where there was once heartache, bitterness, loneliness, and love for self, I began to discover an everlasting friendship with Jesus, which would give me peace, hope and love for others, even for my enemies.

"For God so loved me that He gave His only begotten Son, that believing and trusting in Him I would not perish but have everlasting life." For God did not send His Son into the world to condemn me, but that I through Him might be saved and healed. That is how I would later read John 3:16, 17 to myself. When I did, it took on a very personal meaning and revealed to me that the thoughts of God towards me are not evil, but thoughts of good and peace, to give me a future and hope.

For so long I had bought into the lies that Satan had whispered to me, that God was severe, oppressive, unforgiving, and that if I did not serve Him, I would burn in hell forever. That God was withholding from me those things that would bring me joy, peace and security. That He wanted to dictate and control my life through His Commandments, and on and on. I foolishly believed them without ever investigating for myself the evidence found in the Bible. That was all about to change. As wicked and sinful as I was, that night God revealed Himself to me, and not for me only but I believe it was for your sake as well, that no matter how far we have fallen, God's love, mercy, and kindness are able to reach us.

I would soon discover that at the cross of Calvary, God having undertaken my redemption would spare nothing, including His only Son, which was necessary to restore me to Himself. No truth that is necessary for my salvation would He withhold or cloak in mystery. Also, the many times God intervened to save my life, sending His angel to encourage me in my darkest hour, revealed to me that His compassion and love for me is greater than I had ever realized.

My Friend, see page 169 and I will share with you the many Bible verses that relate to the inspiration I shared at the beginning of this chapter.

Chapter 8

A Drop of Grace

"...But where sin abounded, grace abounded much more."
Romans 5:20

t was already 2:45 a.m., but I had to share what had just happened with someone; I could not keep it to myself. I called up a couple that I knew would still be up and asked if I could come over, and they said yes. Shortly after I got to their place I started to share what had happened to me and read the poem to them. They were quite shocked, to say the least. I do not quite remember our whole conversation, but they probably thought that I had really gone over the edge. I probably would have thought the same if things were reversed. After all, I had never talked about Jesus Christ or the Bible; to them I was their drug dealer, nothing more.

On the way home, I started to recall all the events that led up to this night. I did not understand what God wanted with me. I cried out, *what do you want with me? Can't you see the type of person I am?* I felt then that I was to face judgment for all that I had done. Fear and a sense of hopelessness overcame me and I began to cry. Suddenly a thought came to my mind that there must be more to this visiting angel than I understood, a sense of peace came over me. God is so good, He did not allowed me to be overcome with despair because I did not know what He wanted with me or what to do next. As soon as I got home I looked for the Bible that was given to me by the couple who had invited me to go church before. I found it, and with excitement I opened it and began to read. I believe I opened to the Gospels that night, and as I was reading it was like I was hearing the voice of God speak to my soul. Again, I broke down and began to cry. Although I did not fully understand everything I was reading, I persevered. I had to know what God was seeking to reveal to me and what He would have me do with my life. There I began my search for the knowledge of God.

But my problems are still present and real. I knew that the task force that was watching me would just as soon kill me than arrest me. I also knew that it was just a matter of time before the drug ring I was involved in would think to eliminate me. In addition, I had a major drug addiction that I could not stop. All I could see was darkness ahead of me, with the exception of the light that had just flashed before me. Oh, what a dark pit of sin I was in! *Looking up, all I could see was a drop of grace that splashed upon my heart.* My desire now was to know God and do what was right, out of appreciation for the mercy and love He had just revealed to me. But with all these against me, if God was going to save me He truly would have to perform not just one miracle, but several. Over the next several weeks, I continued to read the Bible and share my experience with people I knew, including John my supplier. I told John that it was time for me to get out of the organization and make changes in my life. Of course, he encouraged me not to and said that I would soon get over these thoughts in time.

Then one Sunday morning, after partying all night, I wanted to talk to someone about my experience. One of the people I would party with used to clean a church part-time. I decided to go there. When I got there I noticed that the door of the church was unlocked. I went in and slowly walked through the sanctuary looking around. I don't know what I was looking for but I felt at peace. I walked up to the pulpit and saw a large Bible that was opened on the podium. Then I noticed a large cup next to it that had *"Feed the Hungry"* inscribed on it. I thought to myself that that would be nice to do. I had a large sum of money with me that I was supposed to give to my dealer later that morning. I pulled the money and everything else I had in my pocket and placed them in the cup. I left a copy of the poem that the Lord impressed me to write and walked out of the church. As I was leaving an older couple pulled up and gave me a funny look but I just smiled got in my car and left. I had not given much thought of how I was going to pay my dealer, I was just happy, happy that I was doing something good for a change. Later that morning when John arrived to collect his money I told him what I did with it. He was quite upset, to say the least, and advised me never to do that again. I told him not to worry that I would pay him back, and that I would need another batch so that I could do so. He agreed to give it reluctantly and we parted.

The conviction I was experiencing also led me to return items that I took in place of money from people who owed me, and I apologized for my behavior. I also visited others whom I had caused bodily harm, and many other problems in their lives, and asked for their forgiveness. Many thought I was going off the deep end and thought that I was just doing this to set them up so that I could do something worse, for I was a terrible person. Others mocked, and ridiculed me, but there were a few who, I do believe, took noticed and listened, and that to me, was a blessing. I did not care anymore what others might think or say.

My friend, if you are living your life based on the status quo or on what others think or say about you, it is sad to say but you have become a slave to the ideology of society and the thoughts and words of others, just as I had. "For by whom a person is overcome, by him also he is brought into bondage" (2 Peter 2:19). I had made a choice never to allow the thoughts and comments of others to dictate the choices I was making. To know God and share what I was experiencing. I was determined to be free whatever the cost. I was truly sorry for the evil I had done, and as I tried to reconcile some areas of my life, God's peace filled my heart.

Later I would read in the Gospel of Luke, chapter 17:11-19, about the story of the ten lepers who had come to Jesus for healing. He told them to go and show themselves to the priest. On the way, they were cleansed from their sickness but only one of them returned to give thanks and give glory to Him. The others just went their way, forgetting the One to whom they owed this miracle. Self-image, pride, doubt, and unbelief had stopped me in the past from responding to God's mercy, kindness, and love, just like the nine lepers in the story. I did not want to respond like that any longer. I had made up my mind and I would endure ridicule and criticism. Moreover, if it meant separation from family and friends because I've accepted truth, I was willing to bear all things. After all, why would Jesus forsake me now? He would not! He would give me His grace to face all things. I did not care how many times I might fall I was determined to trade in my anxiety for His peace, misery for hope, confusion for truth, fear for love, and heartache for the joy of true happiness. For I could hear my Lord Jesus calling me, what loss and ruin would come to my family and me if I did not answer. There was no need to be afraid of man, for God was on my side. Jesus came to give me life and that more abundantly (See John 10:10.)

It saddens my heart to know that Jesus is touching people's lives and they act as if it is no big deal, counting a blessing from God as just luck or good fortune. And there are but a few who truly acknowledge God as the One who blesses, preserves and sustains their lives every day. What joy so many miss by not witnessing for Jesus and praising Him for what He is doing in our lives! "Every good gift and every perfect gift is from above, and comes down from the father of lights, with whom there is no variation or shadow of turning" (James 5:17).

Chapter 9

Coming to a Crisis

"For I am persuaded that neither death nor life, nor angels nor principalities nor powers, nor things present nor things to come, nor height nor depth nor any created thing, shall be able to separate us from the love of God which is in Christ Jesus our Lord." Romans 8:35, 36

Little did I know that as I set my mind to walk with God, I will enter into one of the greatest battles that a man or woman will ever experience in life. For no one ever leaves the ranks of Satan without experiencing great conflict with the wily foe. When one is delivered from the enemy's grip and brought into a saving relationship with Jesus Christ, Satan has not only lost a subject but God has gained a witness who, when taught and trained at the feet of Jesus, will then be an instrument in the hand of God to assist in delivering others. The enemy will try to do everything in his power to prevent this from happening.

As God was working to deliver me from sin, to teach me truth and bring me into a saving relationship with Him, Satan was cranking up the intensity of the battle. "For the wages of sin is death, but the gift of God is eternal life through Christ Jesus our Lord" (Romans 6:23). Satan was doing his best to make sure that I received my wages for the service I had rendered to him. When you work for someone, at the end of the week you get a paycheck for services rendered. Some employers would like to delay payment or skip out on paying altogether if they could get away with it. It is not like that when you willfully live in sin. Your employer, Satan, is always anxious to make sure you receive payment in full, which are misery, sorrow and finally death. He especially seeks to expedite this payment if you become a threat to his kingdom of darkness.

I knew it was time to make a change, but I really did not know where to begin. My life was so out of control. I continued to read the Bible, and conviction grew that the things I was doing had to stop, but still I was struggling to completely walk away from my lifestyle. I figured that since I got myself into this mess, God expected me to get myself out of it. This is a common mistake that most people make, thinking that they can change themselves in their own strength. Our Father in heaven is so compassionate towards those that are babes in Christ, "If there is first a willing mind, it is accepted according to what one has, and not according to what he does not have." (2 Corinthians 8:12). God was working with me according to the limited knowledge I had of Him. I called my son's mother and told her that it would be best if he just stayed with her for a while until I got things sorted out. At the back of my mind, I knew that I did not have much of a chance of getting out of this "mess". Although, I had a growing experience with God, I had no idea how He was going to help me. I was struggling with understanding His Word and what exactly He wanted to do with me. I was ignorant on how to call on God for help, but He did not leave me to myself.

One day John called and told me that he wanted to have lunch with me. So he picked me up and we went to his friends' restaurant. When we got there I noticed that it was closed but he said they were expecting us and it was going to be a private lunch. Although I think I knew what these people were up to, I believed God would protect me. Someone let us in and directed to a booth on the back corner of the room. We sat down, placed our order and as we waited we started talking about things that had been going on. Our food came and we began to eat. I was about half way done when I noticed that my food tasted a little funny. I noticed too that John was watching me as if expecting something to happen. The thought flashed through my mind that they might have put something in my food. I stopped eating for a moment but continued talking. John then called for the waiters and cook to come out to our table. As they approached the table, I did not know what to expect. John then told me to share with them of my encounter that I had with God. As I did so I could see them listening intently but at the same time they had this puzzled look upon their faces. John noticed that I had not finished my food and encouraged me to do so but I said I had enough. He motioned for them to go back to work and then we left. I did not say much on the ride home as I was just thinking about what had happened. I believe God has graciously intervened on my behalf and again saved my life.

Over the next several months, I totaled a vehicle in an accident that should have taken my life, escaped what appeared to be another hit, and was arrested for grand theft auto which should have gotten me many years in prison and, all throughout this time the spirits who I thought were my friends started to torment me. And while serving time for my crime of theft I went through severe drug withdraw. I was then sent to a lock-down rehab center for treatment, after which I was released with time served for my crime.

One author stated, *"Not without a struggle does Satan allow the kingdom of God to be built up in the earth. The forces of evil are engaged in unceasing warfare against the agencies appointed for the spreading of the gospel."* Acts of the Apostle p.167. Oh, how true this was in my life and how much more would I understand this in the years to come. These powers of darkness are especially active when the truth begins to take root in the mind of a believer. God's power and grace are always available when we need help. As I look back, I know that angels of God, unseen by mortal eyes, were sent to aid and encourage me during these months. For Jesus does not reveal Himself to someone only to leave him or her to fight the battle of evil alone. For He Himself has said, "I will never leave you nor forsake you" (Hebrews 13:5).

When I was released from rehab I left my house and relocated not far from where I used to live. I went back to hanging around with the same people, doing the same things, but expecting a different result. Does that sound familiar? But I also began spending hours each day reading the Bible, and as I did so the spirits stopped troubling me. They had been friendly at first, but when I responded to God's call and started sharing my experiences, they turned against me. I realized that I was up against more than just "flesh and blood" (see Ephesians 6:10-18.)

As the weeks went by, my desire for a new life continued to grow. I truly wanted to stop doing drugs and wanted out of the drug game but just did not know how to. I asked God to place me in the countryside where I could gain some sort of control on my life, learn more about Him, and maybe write for Him. My thought was that I could stop using meth and cocaine, the hard drugs, and just drink a little and smoke a little dope. I know that sounds dumb, isn't that how we sometimes reason things out? We would just as soon trade off the lesser of two evils rather than be set free from sin altogether. At this point in my life, I would just as soon trade off the most obvious of evils in my mind and hang on to the ones that I did not think were that bad. I thank God that He is not just about cleaning a little dirt off of us, but He is all about total healing and transformation. He is able to cleanse us completely and make us whole. "You shall call His name Jesus, for He will save His people from their sins." (Matthew 1:21). Although I was struggling with so many different things at this time, God's love was sure and steadfast and He desired to deliver me from my life of bondage.

Chapter 10

Lord, Save Me!

*"Therefore He is also able to save to the uttermost those who come
to God, through Him, since He always lives to make
intercession for them." Hebrews 7:25*

One night after partying with some friends, I woke up feeling very sick. I stumbled down the hallway to the bathroom. Thoughts of anguish and desperation filled my mind. I wanted so badly to be free from this lifestyle but realized that I could not change on my own. I needed help. I had hit rock bottom, and all I could see was death for me. I was where I was as a result of my own choices. "Do not be deceived, God is not mocked; for whatever a man sows, that he will also reap. For he who sows to his flesh will of the flesh reap corruption, but he who sows to the Spirit will of the Spirit reap everlasting life" (Galatians 6:7,8). My whole life I sowed to the flesh. However, it did not end there for me, nor does it have to end there for you, my friend. There are also other principles in the Word of God that can affect our life as long as we would respond to His calling and open our heart to Him. "If we confess our sins, He is faithful and just to forgive us our sins and to cleanse us from all unrighteousness." (1 John 1:9). In addition, the Word of God tells us, "Again, when I say to the wicked, 'you shall surely die,' *if he turns from his sin and does what is lawful and right ...* and walks in the statutes of life without committing iniquity, he shall surely live; he shall not die. None of his sins which he has committed shall be remembered against him; he has done what is lawful and right; he shall surely live" (Ezekiel 33:14-16, emphasis added).

With tears in my eyes, I bowed my head and cried to God, "Please help me." I did not understand how He was going to help me or change things in my life, but I had tried to do it my way for many years. I had to surrender my heart to God, and perhaps He could make a change in my life.

The answer to my prayer came within 24 hours. The next day two men approached me at a parking lot. They turned out to be a secret service agent and a federal marshal and they wanted me to get in the car so they could talk with me. I was not going anywhere with them without a warrant. The one agent then reached out to grab me and I hit him, and I tried to fight them off. We continued to fight it out until they finally got me pined to the ground. They cuffed me and put me in their SUV and then proceeded to tell me that they had a warrant for my arrest for threatening to kill a federal agent. Weeks earlier, in a phone conversation, I made threats to an agent who was harassing me and making personal threats and they had it recorded. Of course at this point I had a few choice words for them. Now I knew they could add assault and battery charges to my case as well. This was not how I thought God's going to help me! But later on I would realize it was the best way for me. I was amazed as how God was working to deliver me from my self-destructive lifestyle. Praise God for deliverance!

Do not ever think that God does not hear your prayers. He is ever reaching out to help us but all too often we murmur and complain at God's method. We want God to help us, but we want to tell Him how He should do it. God knows the best way of helping us in every situation! My friend, no matter what you are struggling with, God our Father is willing to help you right now, and I encourage you to trust that His way is the best way. Always keep this in mind. Look back at the cross of Calvary. Our Father loves you so much and places such a great value upon your life that He sent His only begotten Son, Jesus Christ, to pay the price for our sins by dying on the cross for you and me. He took our place so that we would not have to pay the penalty for our sins and die the second death. (See Romans 5:15-20; Revelation 21:7, 8). Since God our Father has invested that much into your life,

I encourage you don't doubt His love, but trust that He has your best interest in mind all the time. Trust in that love that God has revealed to you at the cross with all your heart. When I view the great sacrifice that was made on behalf of humanity, I know our God's number-one interest is to deliver us from sin and to transform our lives through the Holy Spirit, preparing us to live in His presence when He comes back to live with Him forever.

In the Bible there is a story about the disciples of Jesus crossing a sea in a boat. The waves were rough, and the wind was against them. They saw what they thought was a spirit and cried out in fear. However, Jesus spoke to them and said, "Be of good cheer; it is I; be not afraid." His disciple Peter said, "Lord, if it be Thou, bid me come unto Thee on the water." Jesus said, "Come." Peter came out of the boat and began to walk on the water toward Jesus. However, he took his eyes off Jesus. Then when he saw the wind blowing and the waves gaining height, he became afraid; and began to sink, he cried, saying, *"Lord, save me."* Now please note what the Word of God says next, "and ***immediately*** Jesus stretched forth His hand, and *caught* him." (See Matthew 14:24–31, emphasis added.) This is what happened to me. When all I could see were winds of strife and waves of despair in my life, I cried out and Jesus caught me! This is what will happen to you too if you will just surrender and give Him a chance to work in your life to will and do of His good pleasure.

Jesus stands at the door of your heart and is knocking. Will you invite Him in? No matter what your sin may be or what you have done in life, repentance and forgiveness is offered through Jesus Christ. "Him God has exalted to His right hand to be Prince and Savior, to give repentance to Israel and forgiveness of sins" Acts 5:31. "God delights in mercy" and knows that we are incapable of turning from any evil habit, so He offers us the gift of repentance so that we may receive grace to turn away from those things that are destroying our relationship with Him.

Will you say it with me, *"Jesus, save me!"* It is His delight to stretch forth His hand and catch you. However, you must be willing to accept the method of help that He is offering, trusting that He knows best. For me it was prison, for you it may be different. It is often the case that many would have never known Jesus had not sorrow, affliction, sickness and difficulties in life led them to seek comfort in Him.

Once I was finally in the county jail, the healing of my body and mind could take place and while it's not a favorable place and many challenges are ahead of me I will walk this journey no longer alone, but with Jesus with me.

Chapter 11

Doing the Time

"The Lord shall deliver me from every evil work, and preserve me for His heavenly Kingdom: To Him be glory forever and ever."
2 Timothy 4:18

When I arrived at the county jail I was put in an over-crowded holding cell. After a few hours I was move to another cell and here they crammed about 70 inmates into a 24-person cell. It was extremely hot and the air was filled with stench. There was very little air movement from a fan blowing the stuffy air around the cell block from outside the bars. I looked around and saw two showers and one toilet out in the open, this was not going to be good. After a couple days an inmate approached me and told me that a couple of guys were planning to pick a fight with me. When I asked why he said that is how it is, they just want to try me. I would learn that this is the mindset of most prisoners, survival of the fittest. If they find they can push you around, then they will take your food or make you do things for them. Over the next few days I stayed very alert and waited for them to make their move. After about a week, to my surprise, they closed down that jail and moved us all to a new one down the road. Praise God, a little more room and a lot less people to a cell block. But not much has changed even in this one I would find myself, more often than I would like, in a confrontation with someone.

Not long after this I went to federal court for a hearing. During the hearing, the arresting agents made up some false accusations against me. My attorney advised me not to argue with them, knowing they would have to prove everything they were saying. At the end of the hearing, the prosecutor requested that I have a psychological examination, so a couple of weeks later I was transferred to a federal prison in Chicago Illinois. After being there for a few weeks I was taken to the airport and was put on a "con air" flight along with over one hundred other prisoners and flown down to a super-maximum security prison in Oklahoma. After a few weeks I was on another flight, this time to a federal prison in Massachusetts. I believed this to be my final destination as upon my arrival I was placed in solitary confinement for observation. With no Bible to read, I just spent the days in prayer. After a few days I was taken to a different floor and placed in another cell. Here I was allowed to walk the hallways to stretch my legs and visit a library, where I found a Bible. I read this Bible every free time I got and because of the way God made Himself known to me, I thought my name had to be in there somewhere. I know that it sounds silly but it caused me to read every page and to take my time reading the whole Bible. What I later discovered was that we are ***all*** in there. All through the Bible you read of people who had the same character defects, struggles, and problems as you and I have. The stories of murderers, liars, prostitutes, thieves, gossipers, false witnesses, coveters, witches and sorcerers, and proud, arrogant people living sinful lives are recorded there not to discourage us but to let us 'see that the gospel has power to change lives. And as some of these people accepted God's deliverance from their sinful ways, others chose to despise Him and trample upon His grace and continued to rebel and serve Satan. In the end, they reaped what they sowed, and received their wages for services rendered.

It had been over two months since my court date and I still had not talked with a psychologist. I was not allowed to talk to my attorney or make any phone calls home; it seemed as if my patience was being tested. I continued to pray and ask God for help and trusted that He would work things out. One day I asked one of the officers why I was not allowed to talk with anyone on the outside. I told him I had a 7-year-old son that I had not talked to for quite some time. I explained to him what had been going on since my court date. He just stood there for a moment, thinking. He then invited me into his office, shut the door behind us, and asked me to sit down. He picked up a phone, gave me a clear outside line, and told me to call my family. I thank God for His compassion He showed me and for touching this officer's heart. I knew that this was not allowed, and he could possibly lose his job if his kindness to me became known.

A few more days passed and a psychologist took me to his office for an evaluation that lasted over an hour. He asked me several questions and asked me to repeat things back to him that we had talked about. I thought this to be odd, but went along with it. Then he asked me about my military background, and I told him that I trained in the Marines as a combat engineer. He then asked me if I ever killed anyone. I told him that this information was confidential. He asked me if I had ever killed anyone using explosives, and again I told him that this was confidential. At this time he became very angry, raised his voice and said that if I did not answer the questions he would rule me incompetent. I told him to do what he had to do but I would not discuss my military record.

About a week later I was sent back to court. It was quite trying and difficult to bear, but the Lord gave me the patience and strength. "For His merciful kindness is great towards us" (Psalms 117:2). At court my attorney objected to the claim the doctor had made. He felt that I was competent and that I understood the charges pending against me. My attorney then requested that I be re-evaluated. The prosecutor agreed but told my attorney that he would have to pay for it, as if to discourage him from following through with his request. I was then sent back to a holding facility to await my next evaluation.

After the last go around with the psychologist, it was clear that I was not being treated fairly. I then asked God to intervene and help me. I got encouragement from this passage, "With him (Satan) is an arm of flesh; but with us is the LORD our God to help us, and to fight our battles." (2 Chronicles 32:8). This was the beginning of many times that I would learn to surrender to God and let Him lead. A few more weeks passed, and I met with another doctor. He began asking me multiple choice questions, which continued for about an hour and a half. He was going through a book and recording my answers. A couple of days later I called my attorney to get the update on the evaluation. He told me that the psychologist found me to be competent, and that I got a perfect score on the test. The psychologist also told him that nobody has ever received a perfect score on the test before. Praise God, for He is able to do great things in our lives if we just surrender all to Him.

As I waited for my next court date I continued to read the Scriptures diligently, but it was difficult to focus. At times I would have to read the same passage repeatedly, as my mind was constantly thinking about my son, my family, and how my case would turn out. There was seldom a quiet moment, as voices of other inmates echoed in each room. There were 24 inmates in my unit, and it was set up with two-man cells and a small day room. With everything that was going on, it seemed almost hopeless to try to read the Bible and understand what I was reading, but I knew I must press on. In addition to this, there always seemed to be someone who would give his explanation on what the Scriptures were saying, but I did not want to listen to anyone. The Christians that I had met all seemed to believe something a little different from what the Scriptures taught. I heard all kinds of things, such as how the Ten Commandments did not matter anymore; or how some of them do and some don't; how Jesus is going to come and take certain people and leave some behind to face the plagues found in Revelation; how those left behind would have a second chance; that the Bible counsels us not to eat unclean food, as well as how you could eat all things as long as you pray over them. I heard how you would burn in hell forever and ever if you did not serve God; how you could be baptized by just having water sprinkled on your head; that you must be immersed under water to be baptized; and on and on. After all these different things I was hearing, and after reading a book someone gave me entitled, *"Left Behind"*. I was a little confused to say the least. After reading the Bible a couple times from cover to cover I knew that there was something wrong with this book. Why would a God of love secretly snatch away people who, because of their sudden disappearance, a multitude of lives would be lost? That does not at all reveal the true character of God but instead places a slant on His character as Satan would have it. Later on the second part of the series was also given me but God distinctly impressed me to put it away and just concentrate on reading my Bible. Although this series was written by a couple of pastors they made sure they put on the back of the book that is a "fiction." So basically what they did was come up with an ***imaginary story*** to make some money. I knew I would never get the truth from man as I could see so many people being led astray by these fables and deceptions, it was time to call on the name of the Lord. I went to my cell and prayed. I lifted my voice to God and cried out for Him to teach me. I remember praying this prayer;

"Dear Jesus, help me this day,
I am surrounded by darkness that is trying to carry me away,
so please Jesus let me not go astray.
Teach me your words of wisdom;
bless me with knowledge and understanding in a special way.
Show me how to fight off the darkness
that seeks to consume me this day.
Let it not have victory over me,
for I cannot praise Thee from the grave.
I thirst for Thy righteousness and cry out for Thy strength.
Let Thy light shine on my path and guide my way.
Oh, please, Jesus, let me not go astray.
I need Thee in my life each and every day
for Thou art my life, Thou art eternal light and the only way
to the everlasting world that I hope to go to someday.
So please Jesus let me not go astray. Amen"

I also found comfort in the Word of God. "The Lord is good, a strong hold in the day of trouble; and He knows those who   trust in Him" (Nahum 1:7). "For I, the Lord your God, will hold your right hand, saying to you, fear not, I will help you" (Isaiah 41:13). "And I (Jesus) will pray the Father, and He shall give you another Comforter, that He may abide with you forever ... But the Comforter, which is the Holy Ghost, Whom the Father will send in My name, *He shall teach you all things,* and bring all things to your remembrance, whatsoever I have said unto you" (John 14:16, 26 emphasis added).

God promises to teach not only me, but also you, dear reader, and all that would believe in the promise, if we just ask. "If anyone wills to do His will, he shall know concerning the doctrine" (John 7:17). The key to this promise is one's desire to do and act upon what God teaches us. Let there be no misunderstanding; I know that God has given various gifts to men of the faith as written in Ephesians 4:8-14. However, it is also written, "Now the Spirit expressly says that in latter times some will depart from the faith, giving heed to deceiving spirits and doctrines of demons, speaking lies in hypocrisy, having their own conscience seared with a hot iron" (1 Timothy 4:2). The Word of God counsels us, "Beloved, do not believe every spirit, but test the spirits, whether they are of God; because many false prophets have gone out into the world" (1 John 4:1). This is what we are experiencing in our world today. How is it that we have so many different explanations on various topics in the Bible today if we are all reading from the same Bible? Simply answered, men are interpreting the Bible according to their own understanding and not allowing the Bible to interpret itself. That is why God instructs us to test the spirits.

Now you may ask, as I did, "How do you test the spirits of men to see if they are of God or not?" First, one thing must be clear in our mind if we are going to make it through the "gross darkness that has covered the earth" and the confusion that has taken hold of Christianity today. The Word of God is to be our Teacher and we are not to vary from it in the slightest. Jesus said, "You will know them by their fruits" (Matthew 7:16). Also, the Word of God counsels us, "To the law and to the testimony! If they do not speak according to this word, it is because there is no light in them." He who says, "I know Him," and does not keep His commandments, is a liar, and the truth is not in him. (See Isaiah 8:20; 1 John 2:4.) These verses can be a lamp unto your feet and a light unto your path to keep you from the ravenous wolves in sheep's clothing. These verses have been my safety net when I have met many nice pastors and Christians that profess to know Jesus Christ and love Him, but do not stand the test of God's Word. I do not question their sincerity, but it is clear to me that many can be sincerely wrong. Many who believe that they have been educated to teach the Word of God need once again to humble themselves, sit at the feet of Jesus, and learn the Word of truth as it is taught in Jesus.

My friend, keep this in mind: in the judgment, men and women will not be condemned because they conscientiously believed a lie, but because they did not believe the truth and they neglected the opportunity of learning what truth is. All the lessons that are recorded in the Word of God are there for our warning and instruction. To ignore them will result in ruin to us. We may be sure that any teaching that contradicts God's Word proceeds from Satan. I entreated the Lord to teach me according to His promises and also made a special request for some alone time with Him. "Good and upright is the Lord; Therefore He teaches sinners in the way. The humble He guides in justice, and the humble He teaches His way. All the paths of the Lord are mercy and truth, to such as keep His covenant and His testimonies … The secret of the Lord is with those who fear Him, and He will show them His covenant." (Psalm 25: 8-10, 14).

Chapter 12

Into the Hole

"When my soul fainted within me I remembered the Lord: and my prayer went up to You, into Your holy temple." Jonah 2:7

*W*ithin a week I got my alone time. It was not how I expected it to happen. I got into an argument with a couple of inmates, and the old self started to rise up, almost causing me to get into a fight. They called for the officers and told their side of the story; I said nothing to defend myself, and I was taken to solitary confinement for intimidation. Here I had a time for deep reflection but, my heart was weighed down greatly because they did not permit me to have a Bible or even have a paper to write on. I spent the next few days in prayer. Then one day the officer came to let me out of my cell and told me that I could walk around the day room for a little bit and take a shower. As I walked past some of the other cells I would encourage the other inmates in lockdown and pray with them through the crack of the door. Then as I was talking with one of the inmates and told him of my situation, that I had no Bible or writing materials, he then slid under the door a small pocket Bible. It contained the New Testament, Psalms, and Proverbs. I praised God, that He had not forgotten me. I rejoiced greatly, returned to my cell, and began to read.

Over the weeks ahead, my heart ached from loneliness at times, and many of my past sins came to mind. The time had now come to stop playing the blame game. I was reaping what I sowed and could not blame my parents for not doing this or that, nor blame someone for telling on me or because of the circumstances surrounding me. I felt shut out from God's presence because of all the evils I had done. My heart was full of anguish as my sins passed before me, and my mind was filled with sorrow for my evil ways. It was there in that lonely cell that I learned to talk to God as to a friend. I shared my darkest secrets and most hideous sins, making my confession with tears and a broken heart for my behavior. As I continued to pour my heart out to God I was comforted as I discovered the beautiful promise in John 3:16 and 17, that if I believed in Jesus I would be saved, and that He came to save me and not to condemn me. As I read the Gospels I came face to face with God. The closing scenes of the life of Christ show us the cost of sin. It is here that sinners see the goodness of God that leads to true repentance, which is a sorrow for the sins in our life that cause the pain, suffering, and death of Jesus, the Son of God. We are all responsible for the death of Christ whether we were there that day or not. As it is written, "He was wounded for our transgressions. He was bruised for our iniquities; the chastisement of our peace was upon Him …" (Isaiah 53:5). Please read all of chapter 53.

Wretched as I was, I found hope in the Word of God. I discovered that there is no chapter in our experience too dark for Him to read, and no perplexity too difficult for Him to unravel. "All things are naked and open to the eyes of Him to whom we must give account" (Hebrews 4:13). In John 3:16, 17, and throughout the Bible, we read that God is calling out to us sinners to come to His throne and receive His pardon, mercy, and grace in our time of need. What an awesome, loving Father we have. He was willing to give up His only begotten Son to pay the price for my sins and yours that we may be brought back into a relationship with Him, becoming sons and daughters transformed into the likeness of Christ. We can be encouraged even more as we read the story of a demon-possessed man in Mark 4:35-5:20.

After Jesus was done speaking to a multitude of people and evening had come, He said to His disciples, "Let us pass over unto the other side." He gave no reason for this request. On their way, a great storm arises and it seems that they are about to die. However, Jesus was nearby sleeping, resting in His Father's care. The disciples woke Him up and He calmed the storm. As they reached the shore and as they got out of the boat, a man running out of the graveyard possessed by demons immediately met them. In the past this poor creature had been bound with fetters and chain because of his behavior, yet he had broken free. His dwelling place was in the mountains and among the tombs. Day and night he cried, and cut himself with sharp stones. What a sad picture. What was his upbringing? What were the choices he made in life that left him in this condition? In this story, I got a glimpse of the depths of degradation to which Satan is seeking to pull the whole human race. Satan desires to bring people into bondage to uncontrolled passions and repulsive lusts. His influence is constantly exerted upon men to distract the senses, control the mind for evil, and incite to violence and crime. Through his deceptive temptations, Satan leads humanity to worse and worse evils, until utter degradation, immorality, and ruin are the results.

This is so true, as I can testify to my experience. Deceived by Satan, he led me on to worse evils, and in the end I would just rather die than to continue living a life of wickedness and sin. However, Jesus did not overlook this person at all. The story reveals that Jesus was willing to endure the storm as He attempted to reach this man, and thus He was willing to endure all that Satan could heap upon Him to redeem you and me. Also notice that Jesus does not condemn the man for his sins. He heard his cry from a great way off to be set free. This story reveals a love for fallen humanity, and a Savior that will seek you out to set you free from degradation and sin. No matter how dark our situation may be or how far we have sunk in sin this story is clear. Jesus will hear your cry, come and set you free from the bondage of sin, and grant you peace and joy, then send you out to tell the world of His amazing grace.

I read also of the story of the woman caught in adultery and of how Jesus responded not only to her but also to her accusers in John chapter 8:1-11. No condemnation there, just love, forgiveness, and a promise that His grace would be stronger than any sinful desire as Jesus read the sorrow for sin in her heart. Jesus said to her accusers, "He that is without sin among you, let him first cast a stone at her." He then stooped down and began to write something on the ground. As her accusers heard the words of Jesus and understood what He was writing, they were convicted by their conscience and all walked away. Here He revealed His longsuffering, bearing them in love. Revealing to them that God is "slow to anger and of great understanding" not desiring to embarrass them (See Proverbs 14:29.) As it was written in the law that those caught in adultery should both be stoned. They said that they caught her in the act, so where was the man? Jesus could have easily condemned them as well but instead showed them love and patience, hoping to awaken in their minds their own need of forgiveness and healing. The only one that stayed was the sinless One, Jesus Himself. He arose and asked her where her accusers were. Perhaps she glanced up just enough to notice that they had all left. But she looked back down in shame and sorrow for her sins. However, to her surprise, she would hear the most loving words that had ever fallen upon her ears, "Neither do I condemn thee: go, and sin no more." I believe at the sound of those gentle words she looked up into His loving eyes and realized that the same love that said "I do not condemn you" (you are forgiven) could empower her to live a holy and pure life.

As I read these stories and others in the Bible, I continued to see a loving Savior willing to pardon, cleanse and heal the sinner. As I would continue to read of His great sacrifice on my behalf and all sinners, my heart would begin to melt and all I could do was cling to the cross. Then more hope came as I discovered the following verses.

"The Lord is very compassionate and merciful" (James 5:11).

"He heals the brokenhearted and binds up their wounds" (Psalm 147:3).

"If we confess our sins, He is faithful and just to forgive us our sins and to cleanse us from all unrighteousness" (1 John 1:9).

The condition of obtaining mercy from God is simple and reasonable. God does not require us to do some grievous thing in order to gain forgiveness. We do not need to make long and wearisome pilgrimages, or perform some act of painful penances, to commend our souls to God. It is written:

"He who covers his sins will not prosper, but whoever *confesses and forsakes* them will have mercy" (Proverbs 28:13, emphasis mine)

"The Lord is near to those who have a broken heart, and saves such as have a contrite spirit ... The Lord redeems the soul of His servants, and none of those who *trust in Him* shall be condemned" (Psalm 34:18, 22, emphasis mine.)

As the days went by, the more I opened my heart to God by confessing my sins and asking for forgiveness, the more I was relieved. It was as if a great weight was lifted from off my shoulders. I began to experience freedom from the guilt and shame. I have come to understand that although God knows all things, the purpose of confession is for my own healing, and to be cleansed from sin and unrighteousness. Also, to recognize the condition of my heart that I may then ask for the grace that is necessary for the transformation of my character.

One day the marshals came to get me because I had a court date coming up. Just before entering the courtroom, I realized that because I was in solitary confinement I was in a different colored uniform. I thought to myself, *Oh no, they're for sure going to notice and ask me what I did to be put there.* Would I be honest, or would I try to lie? I realized that if I would try to explain to the prosecutor or judge what happened, it would probably be misunderstood and used against me. The prosecutor was seeking to build a case against me as a violent person. I knew I would have to leave the outcome up to God. My desire was to bring honor to His name, for lying would bring dishonor to my Savior and shame to me. The Bible tells us that lying is an abomination to God and that liars will not go to the kingdom of heaven. (See Proverbs 6:17; Revelation 22:15.)

Through the court session I just sat there, patiently waiting for the judge or prosecutor to say something to me about the color of my uniform. To my amazement, it never happened! As the marshals were taking me back to my holding facility, one of them asked, *"So what did you do to get placed into solitary confinement?"* I told him the charge was for intimidation. He just shook his head and told me to be careful and not to get into any more trouble. I believe God closed the eyes of the judge and prosecutor that day so that they did not see the color of my uniform. Thank the Lord! My gracious Father understood I was just a babe in Christ and that I had not yet learned to bring the flesh under His Spirit's control. There is a wonderful story in the Bible, in 2 Kings 6:8-23, that shows us that God our Creator is able to open or shut the eyes of people if He so desires in order to protect His children. What a privilege it is to be a child of God.

As I was let out of my cell one day, I stopped at the cell next to mine to encourage an inmate. He asked how long I had now been in solitary confinement, I told him it seemed like more than three weeks. He asked if I had been to court and brought up on new charges, I told him no. He proceeded to tell me that when brought to solitary confinement for disciplinary actions you have to be charged with a new crime within ten days, or be released back into the general population. Later that day I inquired with an officer if these things were so. He said nothing, but a short time later he came and placed me in a different part of the facility.

I thanked Jesus for the time alone with Him, for the things I had learned, for His blessed protection, for being gracious to me, for giving me the opportunity to encourage others in the same situation, and for not being brought up on new charges. I praised my Lord for the encouragement I received from His Word when it seemed as if darkness would crush my soul, and for placing me later where I could have a little more movement and continue to witness for Him.

Chapter 13

A Brand Plucked Out of Fire

"Beloved, do not think it strange concerning the fiery trial which is to try you, as though some strange thing happened to you; But grow in grace and knowledge of our Lord and Saviour Jesus Christ."
1 Peter 4:12; 2 Peter 3:18

After my time in solitary confinement, I was placed in a cell with an inmate named Paul. We would sit up late every night reading the Bible and sharing with each other. Then one day he said to me, "Look, I have some of these studies here under my mattress that I have been doing called *Amazing Facts*. They are Bible studies based on biblical facts only. I think you would like them." I took them and very carefully looked the first one over, titled, ***"Is There Anything Left You Can Trust?"*** I started reading these pamphlets; they were only about 12–15 pages long. It was truly amazing! It was filled with biblical evidence of why we can trust the Bible. Each one was based on a topic, and they would gather all the information for that topic from the entire Bible. After I finished reading the first study, I believed God had answered my prayer. It was God teaching me through His written Word. Any question I had, I eventually found the answer. These range of topics in the Bible studies covered topics such as, ***Can you really talk to the Dead?*** Do you really go to heaven or hell when you die? ***How will Jesus come back to get us?*** Who is the antichrist? ***What is the mark of the beast?*** What is the sin God cannot forgive? ***What will heaven be like?*** And more. This Bible study also took me through the books of Daniel and Revelation, show-ing me what the meaning of the symbols are in other parts of the Bible. What a blessing! (See page 170-173 for Bible symbols and meaning.)

I had read the Bible through many times before, but through these studies the Bible came alive and became personal. Of course, as I was learning these precious truths, I just had to share them with someone. Jesus said, "And ye shall know the truth, and the truth shall make you free" (John 8:32). I was being set free from the darkness, lies, deceptions, and the traditions of men, and I wanted to see everyone else set free too!

I also have learned that you must humble yourself and lay aside all preconceived ideas when you study the Bible. It does not matter what has been handed down to you from your parents, nor what your pastor, priest, or your Sunday school teacher said, it is all about what Jesus has to say in His Word. For it is written, "Unto you, O men, I call; and My voice is to the sons of man. O ye simple, understand wisdom: and ye fools, be ye of an understanding heart. Hear; for I will speak of excellent things; and the opening of My lips shall be right things. For My mouth shall speak truth; and wickedness is an abomination to My lips. All the words of My mouth are in righteousness; there is nothing forward or perverse in them. They are all plain to him that understan-deth, and right to them that find knowledge." Therefore, "Man shall not live by bread alone, but by every word that proceedeth out of the mouth of God" (Proverbs 8:4-9; Matthew 4:4, KJV).

As I shared these studies with others, some became very inter-ested and signed up to receive them too. We would come together a couple times a day to pray and study together. My time being locked up I no longer considered a curse to me but a blessing. I was being comforted by God and used by Him to make a positive difference in the lives of other people. However, to my surprise, some people did not want to hear the truth from God's Word. This was a new experience to me, to see people get mad and even violent over some Bible truths. Is it perhaps because the truth presented goes against their preconceived ideas, or because it made them feel uncomfortable? The Word is to them as a sword piercing through their pride and self-exultation. It is written, "For the word of God is living and powerful, and sharper than any two-edged sword, piercing even to the division of soul and spirit, and of joints and marrow, and is a discerner of the thoughts and intents of the heart" (Hebrews 4:12).

One particular person in our cellblock was a minister and who had tried many times to get me to believe something different other than what the Bible said. I could clearly see him taking things out of context to prove his point. I do understand that there are symbols in the Bible that need explaining, but I have found out, as many others before me, that by doing a word search in the Bible on these prophetic symbols found in Daniel and Revelation you can discover their meaning, allowing the Bible to interpret itself. I also have come to realize that God's Word does not contradict itself. Although some passages may not seem very clear on a given subject, I found that if you gather from the Bible all verses relating to that particular subject and study them, you will come to the truth. I have learned to accept nothing but a plain, "Thus says the Lord." This has been my safeguard from deception.

One evening, a group of us were watching a TV program when this same person walked up and changed the channel. I said that we wanted to finish watching the program, and as I reached up to change the channel back and he slapped my hand down. I responded without thinking, and immediately I was face to face with him. One of the other inmates told me a fight wasn't worth it, and for a moment, I knew he was right. It was not worth it. If I hit the man, it would just give the prosecutor the evidence she was looking for to confirm that I was a violent person, so I took a stepped back. However, instead of following the example of Jesus that when "He was reviled, He reviled not in return, when He was threatened, He threatened not; but committed Himself to Him that judges righteously," instead of being watchful and immediately praying to overcome the pride in my heart, I began to say things to him that humiliated him. I was really using a different way of expressing my anger instead of just surrendering it all to Jesus. The other inmates could sense that tension was building up and they encouraged us to take it to one of the cells and shut the door and settle things in there. From time to time, if inmates wanted to fight, this was the way they would do it without the guards seeing what was happening. It was not my intention to fight with him, but it was too late, my words had wounded his pride. As I began to walk in the direction of one of the cells, he sucker punched me from behind, and before I knew it we were in an all-out fistfight right out in the open. As the fight progressed, I could feel the rage rising up inside of me. My old self started to rise up and I wanted to seriously hurt him. However, it was as if an angel stepped in between us. Suddenly, we were separated and stood there for a moment looking at each other. I looked around, and I think both of us were shocked that none of the guards rushed in to separate us and take us to solitary confinement. It was very quiet as the other inmates looked on. But my pride was wounded because I did not get a chance to hurt him, as I desired to. I looked at him and said, *"Get eyes in the back of your head because I am coming to get you!"* We then walked away from each other and sat down on opposite sides of the room. I thought to myself, *I sure did blow it. That was not how a true Christian would have handled that situation.* It was here at this time in my walk with God that He began to teach me how to have victory over sin through the power of His Spirit and His word.

As I sat down, the strangest thing happened to me. God spoke to my heart, saying, *"Go over there, apologize for your conduct and offer to forgive him."* The time had come self-image and pride must be put to death if Jesus Christ was ever going to be seen in my life. I knew that the Lord was speaking to me, and I had a choice to make. I did not give much thought as to what the other inmates would say or how they would treat me afterwards if I did this. I decided to honor God even if it meant looking weak in the eyes of others. I got up and began walking towards him; I could sense that all eyes were on me, wondering what I was going to do. He just sat there looking at me. When I got to his table I said to him, *"Don't worry, I am not coming after you. Would you please forgive me?"* I put out my hand as a token of peace; he shook it and in return asked for forgiveness. I asked him if we could pray together later, and he agreed. I walked back to the other side of the room and sat down. Everyone sat in amazement, in total silence, as if they could not believe what they had just seen and heard. One of the guys turned to me and said, *"I can't believe you did that."* I just looked at him and said, *"It was the right thing to do."* Later I would discover a promise in the Word of God that I believe was imparted to me at that moment to honor His Name. It is written, "Turn at My rebuke; surely I will pour our My Spirit on you" (Proverbs 1:23). It is clear that if we would step out in faith trusting God, He would impart the grace to follow on in obedience to His command.

I began to realize that if Jesus is ever going to be seen in my life, I must make choices to follow the Word of God and respond to conviction regardless of what other people may say or do. So many Christians claim to be following Jesus but they live their lives in bondage to the suggestions of the media, friends, and family. They are afraid to make choices for themselves to stand for God's Word, standards, principles and do what is right in His sight. They fear criticism, ridicule, banishment, and even persecution.

We shall never know how far reaching our actions may be when we are willing to humble ourselves and do what is right regardless of the consequences that may follow. The Bible says, "For we have been made a spectacle to the world, both to angels and to men" (1 Corinthians 4:9). "Now thanks be to God who always leads us in triumph in Christ, and through us diffuses the fragrance of His knowledge in every place. For we are to God the fragrance of Christ among those who are being saved and among those who are perishing. To the one we are the aroma of death leading to death, and to the other the aroma of life leading to life" (2 Corinthians 2:14-16). Later this professed minister and I went into one of the cells, had a nice talk, and prayed together.

A couple more days passed and I was tested again. I realized that God often brings us over the same ground again where we have come short to give us the opportunity to learn from our mistakes and grow in the grace and knowledge of Jesus Christ. It was in the afternoon, right after lunch, and I was just lying on my bed, meditating on the Word when I could hear the same man that I had been in a fight with saying some unkind things about me. The old self started to rise up. I began to feel anger building and the urge to go out and engage in conflict with this person again. However, this time I turned immediately to God and prayed. I opened my heart to God as to a friend, and shared with Him my struggles and weakness for that particular situation, remembering that He sent His Son into the world not to condemn me but to save me. I was honest with God, making it clear that I did not have the strength within myself to resist the urge of venting the anger that I was experiencing. Truly, this anger was only a branch stemming from the root of pride that was still in my heart. My desire was to put pride to death and for people to see the character of Christ in my life, the fruit of the Spirit. (See Galatians 5:22, 23.) As I was praying, God imparted His grace to strengthen me. I remained in prayer until I knew that I had the victory that I asked for. After about 15 minutes, I was able to go out and sit in the same area, expressing no bitterness or anger. Praise the Lord!

Today, I have come to understand that the one of the keys to victory over sin is not to focus on the sin itself, but to behold the life of Jesus Christ. His word said. "Behold the Lamb of God that takes away the sin of the world" (John 1:29). Keep this in mind: love reacts to evil by dying to self, yet lives forevermore, while pride and selfishness live for recognition and gain, only to lose and perish in the end.

I see the battle taking place in my mind. God was teaching me a lesson of humility—dying to self, to pride, and to arrogance. Jesus was helping me to understand more about this battle between the flesh and the Spirit. I would also discover that dying to self will be the greatest battle that we will ever fight. This is a requirement that Jesus makes of everyone who follows Him. Jesus says, *"If any man will come after me, let him **deny himself,** and take up his cross **daily** and follow me"* (Luke 9:23 emphasis mine.) Thank God, it is just one day at a time in our walk with Him. I don't have to worry about how I am going to make it through tomorrow or next week.

Here is a poem I would later write which kind of sums up what I just experienced and what I would later encounter.

The Great Refiner

The battle is raging
It appears that Satan is gaining ground
The fire is roaring
The furnace seven times hotter
At times affliction seems to be all I embrace
However, the joy of the Lord is my strength
My Savior stands by my side I am not alone
Precious in His sight, greatly beloved

His eye is on the flame and it will consume nothing of value
When it is all said and done and the smoke clears away
I shall come forth as gold
For He is the Great Refiner

I thank God for the precious lesson He taught me about the power of His grace. Also for keeping me from physically hurting another inmate and getting into more trouble. I would later understand more that the test of our faith and patience should be humbly accepted rather than dreaded.

Chapter 14

The Long Road

"The Lord is near to all who call upon Him, to all who call upon Him in truth. He will fulfill the desire of those who fear Him; He also will hear their cry and save them." Psalm 145:18, 19

Soon I was back in court, where my attorney presented the results of my last evaluation to the judge. The prosecutor was not pleased at all and rejected the results. She insisted that I be reexamined again at the government's expense. I thought this was odd because she refused to have the government pay to have me evaluated the time before. It was clear to me she was determined to prove that I was mentally incapable of understanding what was taking place. Again, I prayed for God to help me.

After a couple days, I was taken by the federal marshals to a nearby clinic. One of the marshals went in the office with me. The doctor took a minute to look over my file. Then he wrote out a prescription and told the marshal to bring me back in six weeks. The marshal told the doctor that I was there for an evaluation and that I might not be in their custody in six weeks. He looked through his file again and began to question me. He asked me what I had done. I told him what I was being accused of. He then wrote down a few notes and told the marshal that he was done. The marshal was shocked; he knew as well as I did that these evaluations lasted much longer than this, and when we got in the hallway, he told me that he would call my attorney, the prosecutor, and the federal probation department and let them know what had happened. Praise God for a witness. I knew the odds were piling up against me and all I wanted was a fair evaluation.

Over the next couple of days it seemed that darkness was closing in on me, and everything seemed to be weighing me down. I missed my son and just wanted to go home. But where would I go? I had lost everything. Then one night the most beautiful promise came to me. I was deep in sleep, and I heard a soft voice tell me, *"Read Deuteronomy 1:30."* I woke up and thought, *that was strange.* I tried to go back to sleep, but could not. I felt a strong impression to get up and read that passage in the Bible. I did not understand this; I had never heard God talk to me like this before. I climbed down from the top bunk and opened my Bible to Deuteronomy 1:30: *"The Lord your God, who goes before you, He will fight for you, according to all He did for you in Egypt before your eyes."* Wow! I was amazed. I thought, *But I'm not in Egypt,* so I went back to read the story of the Exodus and how God helped His children. What a beautiful story, what a loving God, and what a wonderful promise. Later I would realize that Egypt represents the world of sin and that in the story of the Exodus is symbolized the deliverance from sin Jesus Christ offers to every believing soul.

A couple days later I got a copy of the last doctor's report sent to me by my attorney. It was terrible! The doctor said that I was delusional, very violent, that I should be under close supervision and under medication at all times, and that I was a danger to society! I thought, *how could a person come up with all this from a few questions during an eight-minute conversation?* I was calm through the whole ordeal. When I went back to court, my attorney totally objected to the doctor's report. The judge then decided to disregard the evaluation and subpoena the first two doctors to argue their points as to whether or not I was competent.

The night before the hearing, the doctor from the Massachusetts prison who was first to say that I was incompetent, called my attorney and told him that he had changed his mind and now agreed that I was competent. The next day at court, when questioned about why he changed his mind, the doctor said that after several conversations with my attorney he decided that I was competent and decided to withdraw his first statement. God was working. Finally, there were no objection, and a sentencing date was set.

After a few weeks, my attorney came to see me and told me that the prosecutor was offering me a five-year plea agreement with an open end. This meant that if I accepted I agree to a five-year sentence, and the open end meant that I would accept additional time if the judge decided I needed it. I could do this, or go to trial. I decided to sign the papers. After appearing in court and giving my guilty plea, I felt some relief. You see, it did not matter anymore to me if I will do five years or twenty years. I belonged to God, I *"had been bought with a price,"* purchased by the precious blood of the Lamb of God, Jesus Christ. I had made the decision that whatever happened I would serve Him. On the way back to the jail after pleading guilty, one of the marshals asked me how it went. I told him that I pleaded guilty to a five-year open. He was shocked. Little did I know that the majority of the time when you sign an open-end plea agreement they give you more time. I told him I had faith. He said, *"I do too, but not that much."*

My friend, each one of us must have a living experience in the things of God. Our faith will only grow when we exercise it, and we exercise it when we face obstacles that seem insurmountable or difficulty and trial. Unwavering faith in His Word is the only thing that will endure in the days in which we live. Do you believe the promises of God and that He is able to fulfill them? Read His promises with a believing heart, and if need be ask God to help your unbelief.

Soon it was time to go before the judge. On my way into court, my attorney pulled me aside and told me that the judge said that I could pick the prison I wanted to go to as long as it was a medical facility. This sounded strange to me. I thought to myself, *Now what are they up to?* I sat down in my seat and waited patiently. I then heard a call for a federal marshal to take the stand. It was the marshal that was in the room with me the day I got my last evaluation. The prosecutor asked a few questions, and then he was told to step down. I thank God for a witness. The judge then addressed me.

Judge: *"Mr. Page, will you please stand. Do you have anything you would like to say?"*

Me: *"Yes, your honor. Throughout this case I have been evaluated several times, and all that I have ever wanted was a fair evaluation. My request is that if I am to be evaluated again that no past evaluations will be viewed, so that the person doing the evaluation will do so without any preconceived ideas. Also, I ask that you do not order me to be put on any medication. I have been on drugs most of my life, and I don't want to be on any kind of drug now."* The judge said that he would not give in to my request regarding my other records being viewed for the purpose of further evaluations. He then said,

Judge: *"Mr. Page, has your attorney explained to you that you may pick the prison you want to go to?"*

Me: *"Yes, your honor, he told me that Rochester, Minnesota, was a nice place. So I choose to go there."* (I don't know what I was thinking when I said that. As if any prison is a nice place to be). The judge agreed and told me that while I was there I was to get another evaluation. Then he said,

Judge: *"I am sentencing you to 21 months..."*

I was shocked! Speechless! All I could say was, *"Thank you."* Not 21 years, not 5 years, but 21 months.

God is so merciful and is fulfilling His Word in my life. "He has not dealt with us according to our sins, nor punished us according to our iniquities. For as the heavens are high above the earth, so great is His mercy toward those who fear Him; as far as the east is from the west, so far has He removed our transgressions from us" (Psalm 103:10-12). Throughout my case, Jesus never stopped offering me comfort through His Word.

Today, whenever I share this part of my testimony, I can't help but shed a few tears. I know that I should be in prison for life for all the evil I have done, and that I deserve death for breaking God's commandments. "But God gave us a gift that we do not have to die the second death and be cast into the lake of fire "prepared for the devil and his angels," and that gift is Jesus Christ. He is the only way, the only truth, and life.

A few weeks later, I was on my way to my final destination, Rochester, Minnesota. While being processed, I was told that I would be working in the landscape department at the prison. When I walked through the prison yard I felt at peace. It was, as my attorney said, a very nice place, if you can imagine a prison being a nice place. There were fruit trees and beautiful flowers everywhere, and they even had their own vegetable garden. I saw hawks, squirrels, and geese. It had been a year since I touched the grass and been out in the open without being in a cage of some kind. You never know how much you appreciate nature until it is taken away from you. It was a blessing just to touch the grass. Oh, how everything suddenly looked so much brighter. The branches of trees were waving in the wind, the beautiful flowers were blooming, and fluffy clouds were in the sky, all seemed to be giving praise to God.

On my way back into the building an inmate approached me and asked me if I had just arrived and if I needed anything, such as food or shoes. I told him that I could use some running shoes, and he said that he would see what he could do. Later he brought me a pair to wear. I was thankful and I was simply amazed at how God was already working to provide what I needed.

I'm often asked about the living conditions I experienced while inside prison. While the outside area was more pleasant than I imagined it would be, inside was a different story. There was no privacy. There were four men to a cell, which was only about eight feet wide and about twelve feet long. It had bunk beds on both sides with a small desk and cabinet at the end of each bed. It had one window, but it could not be opened. I thought to myself, *that's pretty crowded, but praise God the toilet and sink are in a different room!*

I then took my Bible and went out into the yard to read. It was not long before another inmate came up to me and asked, *"Do you understand what you're reading there?"* I told him yes but that I was still searching. He sat down and we began to talk. I knew right away he was anxious to teach me. We shared for a little bit and he went on his way. Later, when I returned to my cell some other inmates told me that I had two weeks to find a job at the prison. If I failed to do so I would be sent to solitary confinement. They said I was to go around and fill out applications, just as I would do on the outside, but they told me that usually all the new people are assigned to kitchen duty. I told them the processing officer said that I would be working in the landscaping dept, but they just laughed at me. Over the next week and a half I just studied and prayed for direction. I waited until a couple of days before my time was up, as I believed God wanted me to work in landscaping, and then I went to the landscape office and filled out my application. I had an interview and was told to report to work on Monday and that I would be paid 12¢ an hour. This was the lowest paying job I ever had in my life. Thank God they did not take out taxes!

Each day after cutting the grass with one of those old '50s-style push mowers, I would sit down and read my little pocket Bible. I also enjoyed reading a book called **Steps to Christ**. It was this little book that greatly encouraged me in my walk with God. I enjoyed being outside in nature, everything looked so much brighter than I remembered it. The area I worked in had plum trees, and sometimes when the fruit was ripe I would pick some and enjoy it. I continued to search the Scriptures daily. I finished my *Amazing Facts* studies, and because everything was based upon the Word of God only, I decided to sign up for the next study they offered, called *Storacles of Prophecy*. This study went deeper into the books of Daniel and Revelation, and I learned the meaning of the symbols in the book of Revelation from other parts of the Bible. This was so neat, as I could clearly understand the book so many said was closed to our understanding or that only a pastor could tell you about. I also learned later that there are seven blessings God offers to the one who reads, hears and keeps His counsel in the book of Revelation (See Revelation 1:3, 14:13, 16:15, 19:9, 22:7, 22:14.) God was showing me how His Word interprets itself. I could also see history confirmed the prophecies that I was reading about, and this greatly strengthened my faith in His Word as well as assured me that the prophetic events in the future would also be fulfilled.

During my stay, from time to time I would like to play a game of chess. There was one person in particular whom I enjoyed playing against, even though I lost most of the time. His name was Chuck Gibson. He was restricted to a wheelchair and only had the full use of his left hand. He was kind of a wild-looking guy, but I noticed how kind he was to others. He always shared whatever he had, and if there was something that he could do for anyone he would happily do it. During our games I would talk to him about Jesus, and I would share with him how God had done so many things for me. I spoke of how He was teaching me through His Word some really amazing things. But he did not want to hear it. This was a very touchy subject. Sometimes he would start using profane language and tell me to stop talking about it.

He told me one time how angry he was, and if God was a loving God, he wanted to know why He put him in a wheelchair, and why had God killed his brothers. Chuck had been in an accident at the age of twenty-one and as a result he was paralyzed from his chest down. Also, later in life, he lost a couple of brothers. I told him that God did not put him in that wheelchair, and God had not killed his brothers, nor did He put us in prison. I explained this was all the result of sin. It was because of the choices we made in life to indulge in sinful activity, and these were the consequences. He did not want to hear that either.

Chuck would attend a pagan worship service where they worshiped 36 different gods! However, I never gave up. I would pray for him, knowing that it was the will of God that none perish but all come to repentance, and that all be saved and come to the knowledge of the truth. (See 2 Peter 3:9; 1 Timothy 2:4.) I knew that there would come a time that Chuck would have to make a choice and respond to God's call.

Then one day, while playing a game of chess with him, I decided to share again. I started to tell him about some of the things that I was learning from the book of Daniel. I shared with him some things that I was learning from chapter two. How it revealed world history from the time of Daniel the prophet to the coming of Christ. Now this was interesting to him, as he seemed to have knowledge of history. He even shared with someone in his worship group and then asked the whole group if they would be willing to listen to what I had shared with him. Of course, he was ridiculed and they did not have anything pleasant to say about me either. He stopped going to that service for a while but later returned. Chuck and I continue to form a great friendship even though we had different religious beliefs. He also didn't forget the things I've shared with him.

I started attending a Tuesday night worship service. The pastor seemed to be very kind and encouraging. Up to this time, I did not understand why there were so many different denominations. Nor did I understand why some Christians would worship on Saturday, some on Sunday and others on different days. However, I could count on God to make this clear to me as well.

I have come to the point in my life where I was ready to make an open profession of choosing Jesus Christ to be Lord of my life. I was baptized as an infant in the Catholic Church by sprinkling, but being an infant, I had no choice or understanding. I wanted to be baptized by immersion as Jesus was, as He is my example (See Matthew 3:16). The Bible says, "If there is first a willing mind, it is accepted according to what one has, and not according to what he does not have" (2 Corinthians 8:12).

Baptism is a sacred act. It is like a wedding ceremony. As a man and woman pledge themselves exclusively to one another for better or worse, in sickness or health, in poverty or wealth, they make a solemn commitment to live together until death. At our baptism we are making a commitment to love the Lord with all our heart, strength, and mind by accepting Jesus Christ as our Savior, and His Word as our counselor and guide. We are acknowledging "all scripture is given by inspiration of God, and is profitable for teaching, for reproof, for correction, for instruction in righteousness." We are also promising that we will "live by every word that proceeds from the mouth of God," that his Word will be the governing authority of our lives. The question is asked, "Can two walk together unless they are agreed?" Keep in mind we cannot walk in harmony with God if we neglect and reject His principles, standards, and His law. (See 2 Timothy 3:16; Matthew 4:4; Amos 3:3.) I was making a promise that in sickness or in health I would still choose to serve Him; that whether I found myself with or without money I would serve Him; that no matter what circumstances I find myself in, I determined to serve Him; and be faithful to in spite of ridicule, criticism, or persecution. Baptism is all about becoming a new creature in Christ. It is about forming new habits and behaviors that bring me into harmony with the divine principles of love. We are to be "buried with Him (Jesus) through baptism into death, that just as Christ was raised from the dead by the glory of the Father, even so we also should walk in *newness of life*."

One Tuesday evening, the pastor made a call for those who wanted to come forward for baptism. About twelve of us stood up, and it was arranged for the following Tuesday for us to be baptized. The day came and we all gathered and followed the pastor to a room in the medical building where he filled up a tub. One by one, we took the plunge under the watery grave. However, I noticed something very strange happened that I did not quite understand. As each person came up out of the water, the pastor would look at them and start to speak in a strange way. He seemed to be saying the same set of words repeatedly but not making any sense. A few would just follow along with him and start chanting the same way. Others said nothing. When it was my turn, as I came out of the water, the pastor looked at me and as before started chanting. I just looked at him and said, "Praise God and amen." I suppose if he wanted me to I could say it repeatedly, or I could say it real fast over and over until it sounded like what he was saying, but I could see no point in this. I changed from my wet clothes and went back to my cell rejoicing that I was now a son of the Most High God, Creator of the universe, and Redeemer of my life.

Several months passed and it was time for me to be released to a halfway house. I made my rounds to visit those that I had come to know and considered friends. There were only three: Berga, Warren, and Chuck. They were true friends who shared kindness and love, expecting nothing in return. I could see Jesus Christ in all of them, even Chuck, who did not know Jesus yet as his personal Savior. I had prayer with each one of them and promised to stay in touch. I know they thought in their hearts that they probably would never hear from me again. That is how it is about ninety percent of the time when someone is released; they never write back or visit. But I knew that I would keep my friendship to them for life.

Reader, if you are in prison reading this book, I appeal to you. Those with whom you truly bond, don't let them down when you get out; stay in touch. On the other hand, if you're somebody that knows someone who is incarcerated, it would truly be a blessing to them if you would take the time to write them once in a while. People in prison are human beings too. They are just in prison for what? Sin. Have we not all sinned? The Bible tells us we *"all have sinned, and come short of the glory of God"* (Romans 3:23).

As I was walking through the prison gates, a passage came back to my mind that I had just read a few days before. Isaiah 62:10: *"Go through, go through the gates; Prepare ye the way of the people; cast up, cast up the highway; gather out the stones; lift up a standard for the*

people." At this time I did not quite understand what God was asking of me. I just wanted to live according to His Word.

I had a long bus ride to the halfway house; it was cold and windy but it was nice to be outside of prison walls. I pondered upon the amazing grace that God had shown me. Truly the God of heaven and earth is *"gracious, longsuffering, and abundant in goodness and truth. Keeping mercy for thousands, forgiving iniquity and transgression and sin, and that will by no means clear the guilty."* My heart was stirred and tears of joy started coming down my cheeks. "The Lord is near to all who call upon Him, to all who call upon Him in truth. He will fulfill the desire of those who fear Him; He also will hear their cry and save them" (Psalm 145:18, 19 emphasis mine.)

Chapter 15

A New Beginning!

"Seek first the kingdom of God and His righteousness, and all these things shall be added to you." Matthew 6:33

A halfway house is a place where those who have been incarcerated stay to prove that they are able to adapt to society again. I was to stay there for six weeks. When I got there I was searched, had a breathalyzer and a drug test. I was told who my counselor would be, and a meeting was scheduled for the next day. I put my few belongings away and prayed, thanking God for my safe arrival. I then called my son; it was so good to hear his voice, knowing that it would not be long before I would see him again. I was not exactly sure when, because after talking to his mother I could tell she was a little hesitant to let me back into his life, but I understood why. She was looking out for his best interest and had no idea of my conversion experience. We can tell people all day long that we are Christians, but actions speak louder than words. All I could do was be patient, which was going to be a challenge because I wanted so much to get right back into my son's life. From his earliest years, my son, liked to help with whatever I was doing in the kitchen or remodeling work around the house, and we both loved animals.

One of the important things I have learned is that our children really enjoy one-on-one time with us. I don't mean the TV and video games being the third party. Doing things together like canoeing, fishing, biking, and nature walks; camping, doing a garden together, and even cooking is a lot of fun. It is here were bonding takes place during those personal talks. I try to stay away from things that are competitive as this changes our focus away from our growing together. When I look back to the times when there was no TV, video games, or even radio, the bonds between parents and children were far stronger and better than what they are today. I couldn't wait to get him back in my life.

My next phone call was to Pastor Wayne, a pastor of a local church. I had written to him a few weeks before I left. He wrote back, gave me his phone number and told me to call him when I arrived in the area. He did not delay; he came right over with one of the elders. They arranged for me to be picked up that weekend for church. Thank God for His provision.

The next day I met my counselor and she explained to me the rules and immediately there was a problem. She told me that I could leave the facility for only two hours at a time. I told her that I wanted to go to church and that the church service with fellowship meal would be at least four hours. She said that she would have to think about it. I took it to the Lord in prayer and left it in His hands. A few days later my request was granted and I was given three hours. I praised God.

Bob and Missy, who were the elders of the church, picked me up that weekend. Our morning class was nice as we went through a devotional for the week. The main service was a blessing as well, but one thing left me deeply troubled. You see, when the offering plate came by I had nothing to put in. Immediately I thought of the large amount of money I had wasted partying and living for self, now, I had nothing to give for the cause of spreading the gospel, and my heart was broken. I looked forward to the day when I would have something in my hand to give.

I was encouraged by this elderly couple, Bob and Missy, as they told me stories of their experiences of ministering to prisoners. They had so much love for people and enjoyed sharing the gospel. Even though they were both retired, their lifestyle gave clear evidence that there is no such thing as retirement from being a Christian. Witnessing for Jesus is not just an occasional act, but a lifestyle. They were very kind to me and invited me over as often as I could come for fellowship meals.

Again, I saw the opportunity to share some of the Bible study booklets that I had received with other former inmates, and even some of the staff at the halfway house. I remember back at the prison, when one of the officers noticed these little booklets in my room and picked some up, went back to his office and started reading them. When he returned them to me later, I was very happy to see his interest. I shared all that I could with him and prayed for him. I started to notice how people were interested in the truth. So many people have been taught to believe in tradition or have been deceived into believing a lie, that when they receive the biblical truth it really kindles a new desire to search the Scriptures.

My short stay at the halfway house was just about up. I had my first meeting with my probation officer, and he seemed to be nice person. He made it clear that I would be seeing him once a week, and that he and others would be keeping a very close eye on me. I thought to myself, *Good, maybe they will learn something about Jesus.* He asked me if I had somewhere to go when I get out. I told him I had nowhere to go. He made it clear to me that unless I had somewhere to be released to that was approved of I would not be getting out. I began to pray, asking God for His guidance. It was just a few days before my release when my probation officer called and asked if I had things worked out yet. I told him I still had nowhere to go. He then asked me if I would live in a homeless shelter. I agreed, because I thought anywhere had to be better than prison. He asked if I wanted to go back to my hometown, but I told him no way! He said that he would check into things and get back with me.

There was no need for me to go back into all that chaos. I needed a fresh start, a new environment. You see, one of the biggest mistakes prisoners make when they are released is to go back to the same place where they first got into trouble. I do realize that for the most part offenders are sent back to the area where they committed the crime. However, where we stay is up to us. When we want to start new lives, we must change the people we associate with, the places we live in, the things we do. We cannot hang out with the same people and expect to stay clean and out of trouble. You cannot hang out at the crack house watching the game without getting caught up in the game going for the easy money again or getting high. Ladies, you cannot go to the club thinking you're just going to have some fun with the girls. When you are influenced by the music and you have a couple of drinks you find yourself out with some stranger doing just what you said you were not going to do. If you hang out with the same people, go to the same places, I can assure you that you will do the same things that got you locked up in the first place. I know, because it has happened to me before. How many times have you been locked up before? Whenever I asked this question during prison ministry programs, many raised their hands several times because they have been locked up more than once. The main reason we continue to cycle through the system is that we do the same things expecting different results. If you have not figured it out by now, it's not going to happen. It took me three times going through the system to figure it out too. Many reasoned that they have nowhere else to go. God will provide if we ask Him and are willing to humble ourselves and follow where he leads. Keep this in mind: the county, state, and federal government do not have a problem housing, clothing, feeding, and then burying you. They will do it 24/7. Prison walls will not change you, their clothing will not change you, their food will only make you fat, and their medication will only alter your mind. Without Jesus making a daily change in your heart through a daily relationship with Him you will only continue to go through this vicious cycle again and again. We must believe that God *"is able to do exceedingly abundantly above all that we ask or think,"* and that He will make a way out of no way.

Do you have children, younger brothers and sisters, nieces and nephews? My friend, do you want your children to follow you into the prison system? If not, what has to change? You see, if all we offer our children is the lifestyle that brought us to prison, then what hope do they have? None. And here are the sad facts. Every Juvenile facility we have been to so far and had asked the question, "how many of you have had parents locked up before or are currently incarcerated"? 70 to 80 percent raise their hands. So we can say all day long we don't want them to follow us into the system, but they are. Only you can change that. By God's grace I was able to get back in my son's life and he could see a change in choices I was making and it had a big influence for the positive in his life, and I still see it today.

It is time for all of us to offer our youth something better than immorality, corruption, violence and a watered down gospel. The only hope our young people have today is the example of holy living, of belonging wholly to God; a living testimony of the power of the gospel to transform a persons life and sustain it in godliness. Let us make a full surrender to Jesus Christ, not only for our own soul's sake but also for the sake of our children. God not only wants to save us but He wants to save our whole family.

My probation officer called later and asked me if I would stay at a homeless shelter somewhere in Indiana. I said I would, and he said that he would check to see if they had any openings. It was the end of December and was very cold. With only a few days before my release, I was praying earnestly for God to provide a place for me. I was clinging to the promises in Matthew 6:33 and Philippians 4:19, also searching my heart to be sure that I was fulfilling the conditions laid down in His Word. The promise would be fulfilled according to God's will, His way, and in His time. A few days later my probation officer informed me that the staff at the shelter would hold a bed for me. Praise God.

Well, the day finally came, December 31, 2002, New Year's Eve. What a blessing to get out and start a new life at the beginning of the year! My probation officer picked me up, gave me a ride to the shelter, and stayed with me while I checked in. Again, God had blessed. This place, to my understanding, is one of the nicest homeless shelters in the country. It not only provides beds and food, but it also offers many educational programs. Its goal is to help people get back on their feet. At first I wanted to hurry up and get a job so that I could get back on my own and get my son back in my life, but God had another plan. This passage would often come to mind: *"Rest in the Lord, and wait patiently for Him"* (Psalm 37:7). My lesson in patience was about to grow.

I met with *Catherine*, a case manager, to discuss my goals. She seemed nice and wanted to help. She told me that it would be beneficial for me to go through the educational programs provided by the shelter before looking for a job. The programs would last only about three months, so I agreed. Shortly after starting the programs, the Lord provided a part-time job of shoveling snow at night. This was a fulfillment of the counsel and promise in Psalm 37:4: "Delight yourself also in the Lord, and He shall give you the desires of your heart."

A week passed, and I wanted to go to church. I had a little directory sent to me from the Bible school that gave me a list of churches in the area. I noticed two churches on the map, and I recognized one of the street names. I figured it would be best if I walked to the church on Friday to time myself so I could see how long it would take to get there. I did not want to be late and miss any of the services. A person I met at the shelter agreed to come along with me. I have never been good with directions so it was up to God to guide my way. I think it was only about 15 degrees that morning so we dressed warm and started walking. After walking for about five blocks, I thought we should have come across the street we were looking for, and when we didn't I knew we had gone in the wrong direction. Then I saw a street sign I remembered from my directory, and there was also a church on this street. We headed down that street, hoping to find it. After walking for about an hour, it seemed we would never find it. Our hands and feet started to get pretty cold, and my friend suggested that we give up because there seemed to be nothing but houses. Being persistent, I encouraged him to go a little further, and finally about a half hour later we found the church (little did I realized we actually walked to the next town.) Just as we arrived, someone was pulling up. We inquired about the time for services and they handed us a bulletin. I praised God all the way home.

We started out early the next morning and although it was very cold, I knew that the hour and a half walk would be worth it. When we got there we went in to find a seat at the front pew. I wanted to be able to hear everything the preacher would say so I could take down notes and compare it with the Bible later. I wanted to make sure they also were holding to the whole Bible as the only authority of teaching. I had heard of some churches disregarding the Old Testament, which is absurd because many of the quotes in the New are from the Old. When Jesus was quoting scripture He was quoting from the Old Testament. That day the church was having what I know now to be a communion service. This practice was first instituted by Christ before His crucifixion. (See 1 Corinthians 11:23-26.) However, this was all new to me and as the deacon passed by with the plate of pieces of bread I took one and started to place the bread in my mouth, when out from the corner of my eye I noticed that the others seemed to be waiting for something. I slowly lowered my hand. I think my friend was laughing at me, he knew we were to wait for the pastor to read from the Bible. And when the pastor did, we ate the bread. Then they passed the fresh grape juice around in little cups, and after a reading from the Bible then we drank it. Then they offered another part of the service called the foot washing. I remember this example of humility Jesus gave to His disciples (See John 13:3-17). The whole service was a real blessing. Afterwards a couple came up and introduced themselves and offered to give us a ride home when they found out that we walked to church and were living in a homeless shelter. From that point on, someone always picked me up and anybody else who wanted to go.

Shortly after I started attending church, they decided to hold a series of evangelistic meetings. I was so excited and I invited many of the people I had just met and arranged with a couple from the church named Bob and Eva for transportation. They were an older couple who grew very fond of me and have treated me like a son. They were very faithful and made sure everyone had a ride. About eight people showed interest and started coming. It was exciting watching them learn about the love of God and learn how to study their Bible. After the meetings, a couple got baptized and later got married and began bringing their three children to church with them. Five others also continued to attend church on a regular basis. This really increased my desire to share, as I was seeing more people set free by the love of God and the truths in His Word.

Over the next three months, I attended classes at the shelter and spent most of my free time in study and prayer. I finished my classes and started to search for a job. I was just looking for something to generate some cash to clear debt and get a fresh start. I thought about going back to school and working part time; however, God had a different plan. It was quite difficult finding a job. I found that No one wanted to hire a convicted felon, even a repentant one. You may ask, *"Why tell them about it?"* Well, if you have ever filled out a job application you will be asked if you ever been convicted of a felony. I would always be honest and write yes, since lying is an abomination in the eyes of God. In addition, a false witness will be punished, and those that speak lies shall perish. (See Proverbs 6:16-17, 12:22, and 19:9.) It is my desire to bring honor to God by being honest, even if the results are unfavorable to me. I know that in the end God will bless in His way and time. Since

I answered yes on the applications, I was often asked to explain. After trying to write out a brief explanation on the first few applications, I tried something else and would put *"I will explain in the interview"* on the application. This never worked either. They would listen to me explain myself in the interview and tell me that they would call me, but the expressions on their faces told me that my application was going in the trash. No one wanted to give me a job because of my record. That was ok because I knew that God had a plan, and I continued to take it to Him in prayer.

Then one morning at church while sharing with an elder my experiences in seeking a job, he asked if I had any construction work experience. I told him that I had taken two years of building trades in high school and did some remodeling work prior to going to prison. He told me to come and see him the following week. During the interview, he expressed the need for complete honesty and that he expected me to do a good job. He said that he would start me out at eight dollars an hour. I thought to myself, *Eight dollars? It's been twenty years since I worked for eight dollars an hour.* Some of my last jobs had paid twenty-five to sixty dollars an hour. However, God in His mercy opened my eyes by putting a question in my mind;

GOD: *Dennis, how much did you make at your last job in prison?*

Me: *That's right, Lord, it was only twelve cents an hour for cutting the grass and they were kind enough not to take out taxes. Thank you, Lord, for this blessing and the nice raise!*

God is long-suffering with us as we often murmur and complain about the way He chooses to bless us. I was learning to trust God with my future and be content with whatever means the Lord placed in my hands. After all, God promised to supply all my needs, not my wants. My employer picked me up for work a few times then gave me a mountain bike to ride to his shop. I enjoyed my job and felt blessed for the opportunities to share my faith with customers. I would always pray for the right time and the right thing to share. One day I went out to get my bike that was chained to a bike rack, and to my surprise, someone had taken off my back tire. I thought to myself, *now that's a hard-up person that really needs help; stealing from a homeless person.* That's low. I went inside and prayed for the person that God would lead them to Jesus and then called my employer. I got a new tire, but this time I made sure that I locked everything together.

Days later on my way to work, I saw an old station wagon for sale by the side of the road. I had been accustom to driving a Jaguar and other nice vehicles in the past, so this was a huge change for me, it would be an upgrade from my current transportation. And I was at peace, my life was no longer about image. All I needed was to get from point A to point B, so I inquired about the car and my employer offered to lend me the money to get it. They wanted six hundred dollars for it but we offered four hundred and fifty and they accepted, praise God. It was a good vehicle, clean inside, and it ran well.

Shortly after I started work, I was able to move from the dorm living quarters to the transitional area where two people shared a room. This was a huge blessing as this allowed me to have more quiet time to study and pray. Soon someone from the church I was attending offered a place for me to stay, I thanked him for his kindness but I declined politely, choosing to wait on the Lord. I have learned to wait on my heavenly Father to guide and direct my life. I was no longer attracted by comfort but I had and still do have a burning desire to share the word of God to those in need in all walks of life.

Chapter 16

Tested on Little Things

"Better is a little with righteousness,
than vast revenues without justice." Proverbs 16:8

ne day I had a meeting with my case manager and as she looked over my progress report she noticed that I was not meeting my required amount of savings. The shelter required that when I started working I was to put seventy-five percent of my income away. As she reviewed my outgoing expenses, she noticed that I was giving ten percent of my income to the church, and a small offering as well. She started to tell me that she did not think I should be doing this, and that God would understand if I did not pay my tithes. I said to her kindly, *I don't think you understand. If it was not for God, I would not even be alive today.* She insisted that I needed to be saving as much as possible, and that if I did not apply myself to the requirements that they would have to ask me to leave the shelter for seven days as a disciplinary action. I then explained to her that according to the Word of God, the Lord requires that all people return ten percent of their earnings to Him and in doing so we will receive a blessing. "Bring ye all the tithes into the storehouse, that there may be meat in Mine house, and prove me now herewith, saith the Lord of hosts, if I will not open you the windows of heaven, and pour you out a blessing, that there shall not be room enough to receive it" (Malachi 3:10, KJV). I told her that they could do whatever they thought was necessary but I was not going to compromise my faith or go against my conscience.

It was clear in my mind that it is better to live in poverty with God's blessing than to live in comfort knowing that you will soon face the judgment of God for willfully breaking the eighth commandment, "Thou shall not steal." "Will a man rob God? Yet you have robbed Me! But you say, in what way have we robbed You? In tithes and offerings" (Malachi 3:8). Many Christians think that Jesus omitted this in the New Testament and they will site Matthew 23:23. However, if you read this carefully you'll understand that Jesus was just pointing out to the scribes and Pharisees what they were overlooking. He tells them that they "have neglected the weightier matters of the law; justice and mercy and faith." Remember God does not change. He has instituted the system of tithing as a principle of trust and a way of sustaining the spreading of the gospel. When we withhold from God what He is asking from us, we are in essence robbing Him from the opportunity to bless us. I am not just talking about financially, but also physically and spiritually.

Our faith in God will grow as we joyfully give as He has asked. Again all God wants to do is bless us. However, He cannot bless disobedience no more than we could bless a rebellious child less we encourage them in their rebellious ways.

At the end of our conversation, she decided that due to my persistence in this matter she would allow me to stay. I thank God for granting me the grace to be faithful and the opportunity to witness of His goodness.

Often I would spend time in the chapel and would ask God to lead someone to go in there with whom I could have prayer and fellowship with. I've met a lot of hurting people. Some were struggling with addiction, some had been abused, and others struggled with making the right choices, but they all had a common need. They all needed Jesus in their lives in order to be free from guilt, shame, and sin, and to experience true peace, happiness and healing. I was learning why God wanted me to be patient and wait on Him. I was truly blessed as I took the time to encourage others and pray with them. Because of my past I could relate with many of their sufferings. One time a man approached me when I was in the chapel. He asked if I could pray for him because he was about to have a meeting with his counselor. He just failed a drug test and the policy of the shelter is that if you tested positive for drugs or alcohol you would be kicked out for 7 days. It happened to be winter time and he was in despair. So I prayed that God will move on the counsellor's heart to give *Steven another chance and to show him that God loves him and cares for him; I ended the prayer with asking for His will to be done and in Jesus' name. He thanked me and went to his meeting. Shortly he came back filled with joy and told me that he was given another chance. His counsellor said in the meeting that he wanted to kick him out but there was something holding him back. We prayed again and I gave thanks to God for His mercy and love that He was revealing to Steven. I encouraged him to take time to know God through His Word and prayer.

The more I shared the more I learned. This was a fulfillment of the promise in Proverbs 11:25, *"He who waters will also be watered himself."* And *"Give and it will be given unto you"* (Luke 6:38). I have found this to be the key to spiritual growth. As we apply what we have learned and share these things with others the Lord graciously gives more.

Another time I was in the chapel, when two men came in and they started sharing about the Bible. At the end of the service they asked if people would like to come forward for prayer. I stayed seated and watched others go up front. We all bowed our heads and they began to pray. Then I heard them do the same strange chanting, as did the pastor who baptized me in prison. I just sat there praying to God to protect me from any evil spirit that they might be inviting ignorantly or willfully, because I had no idea what they were saying. I stayed behind as everyone else left and I asked the men what they were saying when they were praying. They said that they were praying in tongues and asked me if I would like them to lay hands upon me and give me this gift. I started to ask them some questions regarding speaking in tongues but they could not give me any Bible scripture to support what they were saying. They seemed to be confused as I continued to ask them about different scriptures that talk about this subject, such as it being in a known language, mentioned in Acts 2. Also, in the Bible it mentions that it is a sign for them that believe not, and that it should only be done by two or three and one should interpret, and if there is none to interpret what the Word of God says, let them keep silence in the church. (See all of 1 Corinthians 14.) They did not even open their Bibles they just packed up and left.

One day, God showed me something that I didn't know existed in my heart. After I had come home from work I got cleaned up, ate and went to the T.V. area. We only had one area dedicated to entertainment, and every couple nights they would play a movie selected by the staff. I was tired and I just wanted to relax. That night was showing an action-packed movie, stimulating and exciting with lots of drama and suspense. As usual whenever I watched one of these I was captivated by it all. After it was over I went back to my dorm and began to read where I had left off in the Bible. I am always amazed at God's timing. I was reading the 33rd chapter of Isaiah. When I came to verse 14 the prophet was asking a question in be half of God. "Who among us shall dwell with the devouring fire? Who among us shall dwell with everlasting burnings?" That caught my attention and I thank God that I did not have to wait long for the answer as I found it in the next verse. "He who walks righteously and speaks uprightly, he who despises the gain of oppressions, who gestures with his hands, refusing bribes, *who stops his ears from hearing of bloodshed and shuts his eyes from seeing evil."* I could hear God very clearly on last part of verse 15 speaking to my heart as usual saying to me "son it is things like this that separate us." I started to understand at this point in my relationship with my heavenly Father that he was calling me to abstain from willfully permitting evil suggestions such crime, violence, and immorality to come into my mind. By beholding we become changed (See 2 Corinthians 3:18). A bible principle that the Satan knows works both ways. We are to set no wicked thing before our eyes and to abstain from all appearance of evil (See Psalms 101:3, 1 Thessalonians 5:22.) God was revealing to me that I was to live in the world but not be of the world (See James 4:4).

As a Christian I needed to ask myself, do the things I partake of promote good or evil? Does it help my relationship with Jesus or does it draw me away from Him? Does it endorse the character traits of Satan, such as murder, lying, hatred, adultery, and covetousness? Does it promote witchcraft, immoral living such as fornication and homosexuality, and teach me to rebel against God? Satan has his signature on much of the media today. The TV, internet, video games, books and magazines are filled with violence and immorality. Much of it endorses the character and attributes of Satan. God's Word says, "Whatsoever things are true, honest, pure, lovely, of good report, virtu- ous/of moral goodness, or praiseworthy/giving honor to God we are to think on these things." (See Philippians 4:8.) This is the standard, not what society sets up.

I had now been living at the shelter for almost one year and had saved enough money to move into a place of my own. My employer and I had become good friends. His daughter was moving out west and had a house she wanted to sell. He offered it to me on a land contract, and the price was a blessing. I moved in that winter and rejoiced greatly, as I now had a place for my son to come and stay with me. Through- out that year the Lord had fulfilled many of His promises in my life. Although there were difficulties and trials, my loving Savior had seen me through them all. In Matthew chapter six, Jesus made it clear to me not to worry about my needs, that just as our heavenly Father feeds the fowls of the air He too would take care of me because we are of more value to Him. He then laid down the condition upon which the promise was to be fulfilled in my life. "But seek first the kingdom of God and His righteousness, and all these things shall be added to you" (Matthew 6:33). I had learned to trust in the Lord with all my heart, not leaning upon my own understanding, and to seek out His will in His Word through daily prayer. In addition, I was acknowledging God in all things and humbled myself to receive reproof and correction, and instruction and guidance was given in all aspects of my life. He comforted my anxious thoughts and imparted perfect peace as I kept my mind upon Him. As I delighted myself in the Lord, keeping my heart fixed upon His Word, He was fulfilling the desires of my heart.

My friend, God is no respecter of persons. What He did for me, and is still doing, He will do for you if you but trust in Him.

Let us keep in mind that He never promised being a Christian would bring ease, comfort, and riches in this life. But He did promise peace, rest, strength, and courage, for the days ahead (See Matthew 11:28-30; John 14:27; Isaiah 26:3, 40:31, 41:10 & 13; Philippians 4:13; Joshua 1:9; John 14:16-18; Hebrews 13:5.) At times we may go hungry. We may be poorly clothed or homeless. We may be criticized, beaten, imprisoned, and even put to death. We may be required to bear all these for the sake of being obedient to His Ten Commandments and revealing the character of Jesus Christ to the world. However, the reward is great! We will have freedom from guilt and shame caused by sin, the privilege of reflecting His character and being a child of God, and at the second coming of Christ, honor and glory in the kingdom of heaven, and immortality. Truly I believe when we all get to heaven and see what God has in store for us we shall all say with joy, "heaven was cheap enough".

Chapter 17

Answers to Prayers

"My God shall supply all your needs according to His riches in glory by Christ Jesus. Now this is the confidence that we have in Him, that if we ask anything according to His will, He hears us. And if we know that He hears us, whatever we ask, we know that we have the petitions that we have asked of Him." Philippians 4:19; 1 John 5:14, 15

Although I went to prison, God, in His providence, directed me to one that had a very nice environment. After that, although homeless, again He blessed. He blessed me with a job and then a vehicle. It was not a high-paying job or a fancy car, nevertheless, it was exactly what I needed at that time. Then He blessed me with a home where I could have more time with my son and be a help to those in need. I realize that God does not bless us so that we can consume the blessing upon ourselves. Sure, we are to partake of the blessing; however, we are to also pray and ask God whom else might we share it with. In this chapter of my experiences with my heavenly Father I would like to share some amazing stories of how He guided, provided for my needs, and answered prayers on behalf of others. I can truly testify that from the time I responded to God's call I have never lacked of what I needed.

I remember a time when after I paid my tithe and offerings I did not have much left. I realized that money for food would be tight that week but I trust He will provide. I was visiting with some friends that weekend when my friend's wife asked me if I would like to take some of the leftovers home. I gladly said yes. By the time she got done packing things up, I had enough food to last a week. Then one time I was so busy between work and prison ministry that I kept forgetting to get a dishwashing liquid. Being a bachelor, I would just use laundry soap from time to time. However, when staying with some friends during a series of prison ministry visits, one morning my friend's wife came up to me with a big bottle of dishwashing liquid and asked me if I could use it. I just had to laugh, and praised my Father in heaven for showing me how He cares for our needs right down to the smallest detail.

One day my car broke down and the Lord provided a dependable mechanic to fix it. While he was working on it, a Christian couple heard I was having car problems. The next time I saw them, the man asked me how things were going. I told him just fine. He said that he heard that I was having car trouble, but I told him I got it fixed. He shared with me that he had a pickup truck that he was selling for $1,200. I just smiled and said that sounded like a good price but I did not have enough money. He just smiled back and said that he and his wife were thinking of just giving it to me. Wow! Praise God. When they brought the truck to my house, I was quite surprised, as it was in excellent condition and was worth more than the money he was asking. It has been six years now and the truck still runs great. At that time I began praying about what to do with my car that was being repaired. I had met a couple at the homeless shelter that was now attending church with us. I was impressed to give them the car. I had just put new tires on it and was tempted to ask for the money for the tires. However, I thank God I did not yield to that temptation. Freely I had received, freely I should give.

What my Father did for me later was amazing. One day, a family who I would visit often called me and said that they wanted to do something for the ministry God had called me to. They told me that the last time I was visiting with them they noticed that I needed new tires for my truck. I thought to myself, *I didn't know I needed tires.* They told me to go to a certain place and there they would have four new tires waiting for me. What a blessing! I was greatly encouraged by this act of kindness, and I was in awe as to how God was working to provide for my need that I did not know I had.

Up to this time I had been living in the city. However, as I continued to study God's Word and received some wise counsel, I was convicted to find a place in the countryside, where I could have more time with God in quietness, to gather lessons from nature and learn to grow my own food. I was learning about the effects of pesticides and genetic engineering that has been taking place in our food supply, so I figured if I grew my own food I would not only learn lessons from my Creator, but have healthy food. (See page 173 for link on genetic engineering and great tips on gardening.) I took this matter to the Lord in prayer and soon an opportunity came up. A friend of mine had a brother that lived in a five-bedroom farmhouse and was hardly ever home. He was looking for someone to stay there for $400.00 a month, and that included utilities. I looked at the place and believed that was where God would have me move. I had to sell a house first before I could move. However, the Lord was already working this out as well. My friend Cary, whom I was buying the house from, told me that his daughter wanted to move back from out west. He asked me if I would be interested in selling the house back to him. I agreed, and we came up with a price that would compensate me for what I had paid towards the home to date.

I stayed in my new home for about two months when the homeowner told me that I would have to move because the home was being foreclosed on. He told me he was sorry and returned my rent payments and said that I would have at least three more months before I would have to move. Now this was somewhat perplexing to me. Why had God, who knows all things, led me here just to move again? As I was praying about this, He brought to my mind that I would not have had the opportunity to meet certain people that I had witnessed to and shared materials with had I not moved there. That was good enough for me. Too often, as Christians, we think of the inconveniencies that we encounter in life and forget about the blessings that we experienced sharing with those we meet along the way.

Actually, this taught me an important lesson. As a Christian, I learned that I am to allow God to guide me to whatever direction will bring honor to His name, for the sake of sharing the gospel to the lost, and bring encouragement to my fellow brothers and sisters in Christ. I have learned to pray very specific prayers as to where I should live, that I may minister to my neighbors. I also pray for guidance to jobs where I may share with my coworkers and those I work for, and direction as to the church He would have me attend to meet like-minded believers. As the scripture says, "Trust in the Lord with all your heart, and lean not on your own understanding; in all your ways acknowledge Him, and He shall direct your paths" (Proverbs 3:5, 6). As Christians, we profess to trust in God and yet we are fearful to allow Him to direct our path for fear of difficulties, trials, and hardships we may encounter. We have been bought with a precious price and though this sacrifice Christ has made we are never to think that He is seeking to harm us through His leading.

I started to look at a number of different places in the countryside. I desired to live closer to my son, where we could spend more time together, knowing that it was God's will that I work very close with him to assist him in forming a solid relationship with Jesus. However, every time I looked for a property in that area nothing was available. Then one Thursday I met with a property owner to look at a place. Although not as close to my son as I would like, it seemed God was directing me to this place. I was very open with the property owner as to my credit not being very good, and shared about my past and conversion story. She listened very intently and showed some interest in the things I was sharing. I offered to give her some Bible literature, and she accepted. She told me not to worry about things and if I wanted the place, she would meet me Sunday to sign the papers. I thought to myself that this must be the place. The following day I picked up my son and took him to see the house. He liked it but said, "Dad, please try again to get a place closer to me. Let's just get today's paper and check once more." So we did, and to my surprise we found an ad for a lakefront property that was very reasonably priced. I made the phone call and left a message. Later the person called back and told me that there were two lake cottages for rent at a reasonable price, but they only had one bedroom. I told him I needed a place with at least two bedrooms because I had a son. He said that he had another place but rent was quite a bit more. I looked at it and decided to go for it. Again, I was very open with the property manager and shared my testimony as well. I was so sure that my heavenly Father wanted me to have this place that I called up the other homeowner to say that God had chosen a different place for me. That following week I got a call back and the property manager of the lake cottage told me that the owner agreed to let me have it if I could pay three months in advance, along with first and last month's rent and a deposit. That added up to a lot of money; however, my Father always makes provisions for where He would direct me. The money was available for me to meet the condition due to the sale of my old home and a new job that I just received to remodel a large home. Praise God. Now I was closer to my son, as I had prayed to be. He does fulfill His promises. "Delight yourself also in the Lord, and He shall give you the desires of your heart" (Psalm 37:4).

One of my heart's desires was to write a book about my experiences with God. However, I did not have a very good education. My English grammar was poor, and I did not have a clue on how to write. But I believe all things are possible with God, and if it was His will that I write a book, than He would provide what I was lacking. One morning while I was still living at the homeless shelter, I prayed that if this was His will that He would make it so clear to me that there would not be any doubt in my mind. A few days later, during my evening devotions, I heard a voice say very clearly, *"Read Jeremiah 30:2"*. At first I did not pay any attention to this. I thought I was just thinking of a verse I had read before. I went to bed, but then during my morning devotion the next day I heard the same thing being said to me again. I then thought it would be good to read it, and once I did I was filled with joy. The answer came very clearly, and I knew without any doubt that writing a book is what my Father would have me do. The Lord made it possible for me to write my testimony and share the things I have learned and experienced so far. I wanted to have something that I could give to those in prison and share with the public, to tell of the power of God's grace in hopes that my experience would encourage people to give Jesus Christ a chance to work in their lives. My Father provided me the ability to write and a way for 5,000 copies to be published. The title was *"From the Cell to the Cross"*. I gladly gave away over 3,000 copies to those in prison, and I sold the rest at a very low price. I did not do it to make money, and what revenue did come in went back into the ministry.

When the time came to print more books I was short a few thousand dollars, according to my calculations. With what I had in savings and from what I could see from my income, I thought I could move forward. Then one day a friend called me and asked if I needed any money for the ministry. I told him that I thought I would be short on reprinting, somewhere around two thousand dollars. He told me he would send me a check for fifteen hundred. Praise God. The Lord was making a way

With a little money in hand and a donation on the way, the Lord gave me the idea to call the publishing company and ask them if they would take half the money down to print 5,000 copies and allow me to make large monthly payments on the balance. It sounded like a very good idea, so I called and talked to the person that worked with me on the first printing. She told me that they don't normally do that, and that a down payment was required and the balance upon pick-up of all the books. However, she said, *"Dennis, I'll tell you what, I have heard from outside sources that your book has generated Bible studies. I will go to the board and make a special request for you."* So we began to pray. A couple days later she called back and said that the board agreed that if I came up with half the money they would print 5,000 copies and would release to me half and as I paid off the balance they would release more. Praise God! I thanked her, but what I did not tell her was that at this time I did not even have half the money. I was just stepping out in faith with my request. I then began to pray and ask my Father to make a way for the rest of the funding.

The Lord began to impress upon one person after another to give an offering for the reprint. My friend Jacob told me that if I could get a donation of one thousand dollars that he would match it. Then shortly later, I was at a prison ministry program and happened to share this with a sister in Christ. She looked at me, smiled, and said, *"Tell your friend to get his checkbook ready."* The next day this dear lady and her pastor came up to me and gave me a check for one thousand dollars. Soon I had all but three thousand dollars. I arranged to begin picking up books. The day before I left a friend told me that he would give me the balance and I could pay him off as I was able. I was so thankful. Of this series of copies I gave away almost four thousand of them to my friend's prison ministry program, called *Christmas Behind Bars*.

After speaking at a church in Canada, a member told me that he wanted to do something for me to help the ministry. After my return home, I received a check for the exact amount of the balance I owed to my friend for the books. My Father in heaven paid for the entire printing and then blessed me with the sale of the ones I had left. Don't we have an Awesome God?

It had been about four years since my release from prison, and I often thought about meeting that special woman God had in mind for me. I had met a few Christian women; however, when I inquired with my heavenly Father the answer always came back, "Not this one." This went on for a few years and, yes, I will say at times it was discouraging. However I would continue to pray specific prayers. I knew the Bible gives counsel against being unequally yoked with unbelievers. However, I also could see that to be unequally yoked with a spouse that had no desire to fully separate from the ways of the world and grow up into the full stature of Christ would also be a disaster. One that had no desire for mission work to spread the gospel would be a great hindrance to my calling to be a true Christian and serve my heavenly Father with my entire life. I had to find someone that had a burning desire to be like Jesus and had no greater desire in life than to go where Jesus would have us go, do what Jesus would have us do, and represent Him in character. I continued to press my petition home to the throne of grace.

At one point in time I registered on a particular Christian website to further my search and within a few days my Father convicted me through His Word not to marry outside of the faith He brought me to. I knelt down and asked for guidance. He brought to my mind the name of a website I had never heard of before, so I got up and typed in the name and, sure enough, there it was. I continued my search for over a year. Just about the time I was ready to give up I came across a woman who was then living in England. She was originally from the Philippines, and as I read her profile I felt the Spirit of God gave a leap inside of me (I don't know how else to described what I felt) I had never experienced this before. Yes, she was beautiful, and I cautioned myself not to let that persuade me. I sent her an email, and we began to communicate. We did this until she felt comfortable with talking on the phone. We would pray and have devotional together every day. Our relationship started out by building upon Christ. She said to me one day, *"Start right and you will finish right."* As we discovered that we both had the same desire to be like Jesus and serve Him wherever He would lead we began to pray earnestly to our heavenly Father for confirmation. Regardless of our feelings we both clearly understood that if our Father said no, it was no. As we prayed specific prayers and received answers to them very directly, we then moved forward.

After we had been talking on the phone for about six months, I decided it was time to meet her in person. I purchased a plane ticket and went to England not only to meet Melody face to face but also to ask her to marry me. We both knew that this was God's choice, and we rejoiced to see each other in person. I called her family in the Philippines to ask their permission to marry their daughter. The answer was, "You come over here and we will talk about it." So, we went there to ask for their blessing and to receive counsel as well.

God confirmed that this was His will with a special gift. A woman named Rachel, who had seen me on a Christian talk show and read my book, stayed in touch with me. She gave me a call, and as I was sharing with her about my situation, she said to me, *"Denny, my husband and I want to do something for you and Melody. I used to own a bridal shop. Have Melody send me a picture of a wedding dress that she would like and her measurements, and I will make her that wedding dress."* I did not know what to say. What a blessing. I thanked her and immediately called Melody up. We prayed and gave thanks to our loving Father for this blessing and giving us confirmation to go forward. My loving friend Rachel and her husband, Boris, sent us a beautiful wedding dress and a tuxedo as well. Having obtained her family's blessings, we were married six months later. Praise God!

God provided a beautiful, God-fearing wife for me. One I could be a best friend to, encourage, bless, and uplift to my Father; one I could trust with my dreams, hopes, cares, and fears; one whom I could love and grow in Christ with. The greatest blessing of all was that we both knew in our innermost hearts that our heavenly Father chose us to be together. This meant that when things get difficult we can never say we made a mistake, because God does not make mistakes. It meant that we are never to give up on each other when character defects begin to reveal themselves. It meant that when trials and difficulties come we are to both submit to God and draw near to Him. Melody's family has a saying that goes like this, *"If you want to speed up your sanctification, get married."* We just laughed when we first heard this; however, we know now just how true those words are. When the enemy would come in like a flood to destroy our marriage we are to strengthen one another, clinging to the promises of God and act upon them. We both understand that we have a choice when disagreements arise, that either we are going to raise our hands and side with the enemy and bring reproach upon Jesus, or take one another by the hand and humble ourselves before God, pray, encourage, and strengthen each other.

Marriage is truly a blessing and gift from God. I have come to understand there are two things Satan hates above all else that God instituted at Creation. The first is marriage, because it represents the union between the believer and Christ, and the second is the Sabbath, which represents our loyalty to our God and Creator. My friends seek the Lord in regards to this matter and do not let your feelings do your thinking. Be patient and trust Him to choose that special person for you and know that our heavenly Father is "able to do exceeding abundantly above all that we ask or think." The Bible says, "With thanksgiving let your request be known to God." (See Philippians 4:6.)

Our heavenly Father opened opportunities for us to share testimonies every time I visited with Melody in England. As Melody and I will take time off work to speak at a church or a prison we experienced challenges as well as God's unfailing hand. There were times when because of the way the speaking engagements were scheduled it put our budget at a stretch, but just in time God would open a way to meet our needs. His Word tells us, "be anxious for nothing, but in everything by prayer and supplication, with thanksgiving, let your requests be made known to God; and the peace of God, which surpasses all understanding, will guard your hearts and minds through Christ Jesus" (Philippians 4:6, 7).

Once my wife, Melody, joined me and my son, we had a small problem. I only had the pickup truck that my Father provided for me, and the three of us could barely fit in it. Melody and I began to pray and ask our Father for a van. We thought this would be the right type of vehicle for us. We knew that we would be traveling for ministry, and it would be nice to be able to lay back in a van and take a nap on those long trips. One day I got a call from a friend who asked me if I would like to do a remodeling job that was about an hour away. I agreed and started the following week. Every day on the way home I would see this nice-looking van on the side of the road for sale. I just ignored it, as it looked like it cost more than I could afford. Then one day I decided to stop to look at it. As I was checking it out, the owner and his daughter came up to me and began telling me a few things that he had just done with the van. I told him my wife and I were praying for a van and why. Our conversation then turned towards God. As I began to share my testimony with him and of the power of God's grace, he began to cry. I thought this to be odd. I told him that I would bring my wife by to take it for a test drive. I took a few pictures to show my wife and then left him with a copy of my testimony book.

Melody and I began to pray about this van. Our prayer was that if this person would accept our offer, which is half of what he's asking for, then we knew that our Father would want us to have it and that He would provide for it to be maintained until He gives us something else. I arranged to stop by that Sunday afternoon and take it for a test drive, Todd and his wife invited us to have lunch with them as well.

Sunday afternoon we stopped by and took it for a drive. I could tell it needed a little work, but all in all it seemed to be a very good vehicle. After a nice lunch we decided to go for a walk. During our walk, Todd and I separated ourselves and started talking about the van. I explained that I was recovering from a back injury and was just getting back to work and, because of our current financial situation, I can only make this much of an offer for the van. Todd stopped walking and looked at me for a moment. Then he said, "I have been praying too, and I think I can do much better than that." Then before I could say anything he said, "I am just going to give the van to you." I was speechless, then with tears rolling down our faces, we hugged each other. He went on to tell me the story of how this decision came about. He had asked his father one day what to do with the extra vehicle he had since business was slowing down. His dad counseled him saying, "Well, son, God has been good to you and the van has been too. You should just give it to someone." Todd told me that I happened to show up that same evening, and when I was sharing with him my testimony, he heard God tell him to give the van to me. What a wonderful, loving Father we have who does *"exceeding abundantly above all that we ask or think."* My wife and I expressed our thankfulness to this lovely couple and took the van home.

Never despair when constant need arises in your life, for these are but opportunities for our heavenly Father to manifest His loving care for you. He knows exactly what you need and is all too wise to give anything that would be a hindrance to your salvation. Press your petitions home to the throne of grace and persevere and watch your relationship grow with Jesus like never before.

My friend, never forget the price our heavenly Father has placed upon you when He gave up His only begotten Son. This has been the deciding factor in me being content and thankful in whatever situation I find myself. He promised to be my Shepherd and that I would not want, that He would provide for my every need and that no good thing would He withhold from me if I walk according to His word, and that I would be blessed for trusting in Him. (See Psalm 23:1; Philippians 4:19; Psalm 84:11, 12.) In these verses I understand that we will have what is necessary for us to grow up in Christ, what it takes to sustain our life, and the resources needed for us to fulfill our part in His plan to share the gospel. What brought these verses home to my mind was a time when a person I was working for told me that they did not have any more work for me to do. My family and I had just moved to another home in the country where God had led us. As we took our request to God for work, He provided. I started getting calls for remodeling work, and I would have work for a week or so at a time. When we would see that I only had a couple days of work left we would ask our loving Father again for a blessing. Often within a day I would receive a call for more work. God has never let me down.

Since I have been out, God has given me the chance to help others along the way. Through the years He has opened up opportunities for me and my wife to speak at churches in different parts of the country as well as in Canada, and England. We also have been invited to speak at schools, to share our testimony and to warn the youth of the follies of drugs and other enslaving habits. Also for several years, we have partnered with my good friend Lemuel Vega and his wife Donna, of *Christmas Behind Bars* doing prison ministry in juvenile, county and even state prisons. My heart overflows with gratitude and praise to God for what He has done.

My life now is more abundant than it ever has been. God teaches us to walk by faith, not blindly, but trusting in the evidence that He has provide in His Word. Not one promise that He has made available to us in His Word is left undone.

Chapter 18

Reconciled at Last!

"Now this is the confidence that we have in Him, that if we ask anything according to His will, He hears us." 1 John 5:14

One day while I was reading 1 John 5:14, I got me concerned about the salvation of my loved ones and people I have met over the years, and a thought came to my mind. What would happen if I prayed for the will of God as revealed in the Bible? I decided to give it a try. I started to do this for my friend Chuck, whom I've met in prison. You see, after I had left prison I stayed in touched with him. I would pray for him daily, asking my heavenly Father to reveal Himself to him. Jesus tells us, "no one can come to Me unless the Father who sent Me draws him" (John 6:44). "For this is good and acceptable in the sight of God our Savoir; who will have all men to be saved and to come unto the knowledge of the truth" (1 Timothy 2:3, 4). I asked God to do all this for my friend. That He would pour out His Spirit upon Chuck and draw him to Jesus so that he would know the "only true God and Jesus Christ whom He has sent." That he would "be saved and come to the knowledge of the truth."

Within three months of my release, I got a call from Chuck. He started to tell me of a dream he had and then asked me very seriously, *"Dennis, I want to know, is God real?"* I said, *I can tell you all day long that God is real but until you have experienced Him for yourself you will never know. I'll tell you what I will do. I am going to send you some*

Bible studies. Promise me that you will go through the whole set and then you tell me if God is real or not. He said, "I don't read very well." I told him that I have the same problem, but that I would pray for him and get people at my church to pray for him too. He promised to do the Bible studies. I think it was about six weeks later when he called me again and said, *"You know what?"* I could sense his excitement. *"I just got baptized!"* I cried tears of joy! I said to him that if that would have been the only reason for me going to prison, it was worth it. Today we remain best of friends. There is no doubt in my mind that due to someone else praying for me, God revealed Himself to me. I have seen it happen in Chuck's life through my prayers on his behalf. This inspired me to start praying more scripture prayers that indicate the will of God. I made a prayer book and started to pray daily, mentioning people by name. I believe that God wants to save us by families, so I started to really focus on intercessory prayer for my family as well as others.

One rainy day while at work, I received a call from my mother's best friend. She told me that she wanted to give her life back to Jesus and asked for some Bible studies. She went on to tell me that my mother did not understand why every time she and I would talk I would bring up Jesus. How could I be such a different person than who I used to be? This particular question often came to her mind. I had never really shared my conversion experience with my mother before but God strongly impressed me to visit her and do so.

Arriving at her home I could see my mother was very tense. I asked her if we could talk and she agreed. I then started to share with her why I made a commitment to live for my Savior. I think she was beginning to understand. I asked her if we could pray together and she said yes, and for the first time my mother and I prayed together. I continued to pray for my family earnestly. A few weeks passed, and my mother called me and said that she had just spent the last couple days praying, asking for forgiveness, and that she had given her heart to Jesus. Praise God! My heart overflowed with joy. I bought her a nice Bible, and offered to study with her. Our relationship has been growing as mother and son. I love my mother very much, and it is such a great joy to watch her grow in Jesus Christ and to see the healing that is taking place through His comforting hand.

Shortly after this experience with my mother, my stepfather became terminally ill with cancer. The doctors only gave him six to eight months to live. My wife and I arranged to visit with him. I began to pray, asking my heavenly Father what to share with him. He grew up in a Christian family but turned his back on God. Although I was not close to him while I was growing up, I still wanted him to know Jesus, that he too could be set free from guilt, shame and sin. That he would know the love of God and have the hope of eternal life.

When we arrived at my aunt's house where he was staying, he was in bed. Due to the rapid progression of the cancer he was pretty much bedridden. As I went in to see him, my heart sank; I could see he had lost so much weight. We talked for a little while and caught up on things, but I was also praying for an opportunity to share with him the love of God and His plan of salvation. He told me that his neighbor had taken him to some church functions and that he had enjoyed himself. Our conversation then turned to the direction I was praying for. I shared with him God's plan of salvation and the hope that we have in Jesus Christ. I shared with him what Jesus had done and is still doing in my life. He just listened quietly and did not say much. He told me that he had been praying and thinking about things, and that his neighbor had been talking to him about Jesus as well. I asked him, *"Dad, do you think you would have ever considered asking Jesus for help in your life had you not gotten sick?"* He closed his eyes and was quiet for a few minutes. Then, opening his eyes, he looked right at me, *"No, I don't think I ever would have."* I said to him that it might be hard to understand but he could look at his sickness not as a curse, but a blessing.

There are many people that would not ever consider praying and inquiring about God had they not come down with some serious illness or had a loved one been near death. Our Father *"is very compassionate and merciful"* and ever seeking to draw the sinner to Christ. It is often in the darkest hour of one's life when Satan seems to have gained victory over the soul that the great sacrifice for sin that Jesus made is accepted and repentance and confession is made. Many have gone down to the grave like the thief on the cross with the blessed hope of spending eternity in paradise with Jesus when He returns.

My stepfather accepted the sacrifice Jesus made for his sins and believed what Jesus had done for him. We prayed together, and I left him a few pamphlets to encourage him. My wife and I stayed for a few days and returned home. I stayed in contact with him, and we would often pray together over the phone. He expressed his desire to change his lifestyle and confessed that he did not have the power to do it alone. I assured him that Jesus would help and make a way for him, encouraging him to continue to press his prayers home to the throne of grace and take his relationship with God one day at a time. My mother and siblings agreed to take turns to go down and visit. Then one day my mother called me and said, "I don't know why he is hanging on, he is in so much pain. He does not recognize some of us anymore; however, he did ask for you. Please come soon." My wife and I prayed that God would touch his mind and grant him the ability to recognize us and understand what we would be sharing with him. Up to this time I had been praying for some type of assurance that he was responding to the work of the Holy Spirit. I wanted him to be there on resurrection day to see Jesus come in the clouds of glory and ascend up to meet Him and ever be with the Lord. (See John 6:40; 1 Thessalonians 5:15-17.) My mind was perplexed; I wanted to know for sure if in his heart he had responded to the message of salvation and believed on Jesus as his Savior.

Arriving at the nursing home, my wife and I prayed again before we went in. The nurse took us to his room where he was sleeping. *He looked even thinner than when we last saw him; there was nothing left but skin and bone.* I gently touched his shoulders. He opened his eyes and just looked at me for a minute as if trying to remember who I was. He then smiled and said, *"Dennis, is that you?"* I gave him a hug, and we got him up so that he could eat. We spent a few hours with him, singing and talking about how wonderful it will be when God recreates the heavens and earth. We talked about how beautiful and full of peace the world will be then, and how we will be able to play with all the different animals. There will be no more death, sorrow, crying, or pain, and the food will be wonderful. However, the greatest thing of all will be living with Jesus forever. (See Isaiah 66:22, 23 and 11:6-9; Revelation 21:1-4, 22:1-5.)

After a while we took him back to his room so he could rest. I told him we would be back the next day to have breakfast with him. Then, just as we were about to walk out of the room, he called to me as if to say something. Then he had this blank look on his face and said, *"I don't remember."* I told him that it was all right and that we would see him tomorrow.

The next day when we got there, he was already up. We got his food and took him outside to the garden. Again, as we looked upon the flowers and little animals playing we talked about the kingdom of God. He asked me what I was going to do (I knew that he meant with my life). I assured him that I would continue to share the gospel and live for Jesus. He smiled and said he would like that. He expressed that he was tired and wanted to go back to his room. We made our way back to the building, my wife pushing him in his wheelchair, and just as I was opening the door to go inside he called out to me, *"Dennis, come over here."* I went over and knelt down by his side. He started to cry. Great sobs seemed to wrench through his frail body. He said he was sorry for how he had treated me and how he thought of me. He asked for my forgiveness. I was overwhelmed, and I started to cry. Years of pain and bitterness were being washed away as we cried together and hugged each other. I too, asked for his forgiveness. Then he expressed the pain he was in, and so we prayed that he'd feel relief. As we prayed the peace of God rested upon him, I could see him relax. We took him back to his room and helped him to his bed. I said, *dad, the next time I see you we are going to walk together with Jesus.* He grabbed my hand and said, *"I want to walk with you."* He closed his eyes and went to sleep. My wife and I could not help but cry again as we got in the van. We praised God for His mercy. In that visit, our loving heavenly Father revealed to us that he did responded to God's message of mercy and that the Holy Spirit was working in his heart. He passed a short time later in his sleep. I know that I will see him on the resurrection day as long as I stay faithful.

One day my brother called me and was telling me about some problems he was having on a job, I could relate to where he was coming from. When a company or an employer treat you unjustly it is hard to beat back the waves of jealousy, bitterness, envy and strife that arise in your heart. Satan will often use people or a situation to draw our minds off of Jesus Christ who is our example in all things. So I talked with him about some of my recent experiences and struggles that were similar to his and how Jesus helped. Over the past couple years as we had been praying for him and he had been asking question about the Bible and this was a perfect opportunity for me to share about the power of God's Word and how grace works in the heart.

I shared with him the counsel "whatever you do in word of deed, do all in the name of the Lord Jesus, giving thanks to God the Father through Him. And whatever you do, do it heartily, as to the Lord and not to men, knowing that from the Lord you will receive the reward of the inheritance; for you serve the Lord Christ" (Colossians 3:17, 22-24.) When I received this in my heart and made it my practice, I received the peace that Jesus promised in John 14:27. When we work somewhere or for someone we are just to look at them as instruments in the hand of God to bless us and we are to do our job as if we are working for God Himself. My experience has been that whenever I applied this Bible principle in the work place it has brought me so much peace and freedom that I was amazed at the power of God's Word. I said to my brother, look outside, do you see all the trees, grass, flower, and the creation all around you? This stands as a witness to us as to the power of God's Word. Whenever God speaks something happens. And when we receive His Word in our mind, trusting and believing, it will do for us what He has spoken, the Word transforms our mind and we receive the promise to the full according to how we believe. Jesus said, "As thou hast believed, be it done unto thee" (Matthew 8:13 KJV) I believe every Bible principle is a promise from God to be fulfilled in our lives for the transformation of our character. This is how we grow into the likeness of Christ. For me this was God's Word in action bringing about a change in my life. All this time my brother listened intently and then he acknowledged this is what he wanted in his life as well.

I realized that people today are in dire need to know and understand that they can be free from sin and the power of Satan. As Christians we are daily given opportunity to share what the Word of God has done for us. My personal testimony regarding this situation I hope encouraged my brother to seek to know God, to "taste and see that He is good" and desire to experience God's grace in this manner also. Prayer was drawing my brother's heart out to God. Some of my family and others in my prayer book are also starting to respond to the drawing influence of God's Spirit. I see and hear testimony often, so I am greatly encouraged to continue intercessory prayer for others.

There is a great battle taking place over every living person. As Christians, by faith we need to join hands with Jesus, who now stands in the most holy place in the heavenly sanctuary, and enter this battle for the salvation of souls on our knees.

There is a powerful example in Numbers chapter 14:17-20 that reveals God answering the prayer of Moses as he interceded for the children of Israel. In verse 17 He is asking God to reveal His power according to how He has spoken. Verse 18 Moses repeats back to God His spoken Word that God spoke to him in the mountain when He hid him in the cleft of the rock and passed before him proclaiming His Name. (See Exodus 33:19-22 and 34:6, 7). In verse 19 Moses is asking God to pardon and in verse 20 the Lord said, "I have pardoned according to thy word." Whose word? Moses repeated the Word of God that God had spoken to Him. This shows us the power of praying the will of God as revealed to us in His Word. Our Lord Jesus is a Gentleman. He will not go where He is not invited. As God hears our loving plea for ones salvation He responds in our behalf. However, I do realize the individual that we are praying for still has a choice to respond to the loving influence of God's Spirit tugging at their heart. But with our prayers in their behalf, the odds of them turning to God increases.

Here is a list of some scriptures that I have claimed in my prayers. As you read them, you can see the will of God for you and for those you pray for. Keep in mind that the words that have proceeded out of the mouth of God will not return to Him empty, but will accomplish what He desires and achieve the purpose for which He sent them. (See Isaiah 55:11.)

First, ask God to forgive them for their sins and show them mercy, as did Moses for the children of Israel Numbers 14:17-20, as did our Lord, Jesus Christ, as they crucified Him (Luke 23:34), and as did Steven for those that were stoning him (Acts 8:59, 60), for God delights in mercy (Micah 7:18). And that the merits of Jesus Christ are applied to their lives. For we have redemption through His blood, the forgiveness of sins, according to riches of His grace. (Ephesians 1:7)

Ask God to draw them to Himself, for Jesus said, "No one can come to me unless the Father who sent Me draws him" (John 6:44).

That they may know Him, the only true God, and Jesus Christ, whom He has sent. So that they will be set free from the fear of death that has held them in bondage (See John 17:3; Hebrews 2:14, 15.)

That they may know the thoughts that God thinks towards them, thoughts of peace and not of evil, to give them a future and hope. That they will pray to God and search for Him with all their heart, for surely He will answer and be found of them and bring them out of the bondage of sin. (See Jeremiah 29:11-14.)

Make the request that just as God wrote the Ten Commandments upon the tables of stone, that He would put His laws into their hearts and minds. (See Hebrews 10:16.)

Ask God to anoint their eyes with eye salve that they may discern between good and evil. (See Revelation 3:18.)

Ask for the gift of repentance to be imparted to them, for God exalted His Son to be a Prince and a Savior to give us repentance and forgiveness (See Acts 5:31) For without Jesus we can do nothing (John15:5)

Ask God to declare His name unto them, that they will experience that the, "Lord God is merciful and gracious, longsuffering and abundant in goodness and truth, keeping mercy for thousands, forgiving iniquity and transgression and sin" (Exodus 33:18, 19; 34:6, 7). "For it is the goodness of God that leads to repentance" (Romans 2:4), for God "is longsuffering towards us, not willing that any should perish but that all should come to repentance" (2 Peter 3:9).

Ask God to increase His divine influence upon their heart, that where sin has abounded, His grace/character will abound much more. (See Romans 5:20.) So that "sin will not have dominion/power over them" (See Romans 6:14).

Pray that they will not grieve the Holy Spirit of God whereby they may be sealed unto the day of redemption. (See Ephesians 4:30.)

Ask God to bind Satan from blinding them to the truth and that his influences in their life be cast down, that no weapon that Satan forms against them would prosper. (See 2 Corinthians 4:4; 10:4, 5 and Isaiah 54:17) "For this is good and acceptable in the sight of God our Savior, who desires all men to be saved and to come to the knowledge of the truth" (1 Timothy 2:3, 4).

Ask that they would be made whole and set aside for His use through the truth, as this is the will of God, even our sanctification (See John 17:17; 1 Thessalonians 4:3), so that thy may "pursue peace with all people, and holiness, without which no one will see the Lord" (Hebrews 12:14). According as He hath chosen us in Him before the foundation of the world, that we should be holy and without blame before Him in love. (Ephesians 1:4)

I am sure that you can add more to this list. It is my prayer that you will experience a deeper revelation of God as you see Him work in your life and in the lives of those you pray for.

Chapter 19

Growing Up in Christ

"I have been crucified with Christ; it is no longer I who live, but Christ who live in me…" Galatians 2:20

I remember a time when I was sharing my testimony with an inmate in my prison cell and he asked me, "What do you want to do in life now?" When I said I wanted to be like Jesus he looked at me and with a smirk on his face, said, "That's impossible." I never gave his remark much thought, because as I read the Bible I can see that there is a creative, transforming power in the Word of God. As I reflected on the character of God, His grace and all that Jesus Christ had done for me I just desired to be like Him and bring honor to His name. I wanted to be loving, kind, gentle, compassionate, forgiving, and humble. I wanted to live a life of integrity, honesty, holiness, and purity.

Even then I realized that I still have so much to learn. One of which is that as a Christian I am to model His example when He said, "Learn of Me" (Matthew 11:29), "If anyone serves Me, let him follow Me" (John 12:26), and "I am the way, the truth, and the life" (John 14:6). Also, "to this you were called, because Christ also suffered for us, leaving us an example, that you should follow His steps; Who committed no sin, nor was deceit found in His mouth. Who, when He was reviled, did not revile in return; when He suffered, He did not threaten, but committed Himself to Him who judges righteously". (1 Peter 2:21-23)

I often wondered, how could I know what was in my heart? The Bible says, "out of the abundance of the heart the mouth speaks", and that "you will know them by their fruits". I realize that one would begin to know the condition of their heart if they will listen to the words coming out of their mouth and pay attention to their actions. How do we respond to circumstances surrounding us? How do we respond to the way people talk to us or the way they treat us? Do we blame God or take responsibility for the choices we make? How do we respond to the trials that God allows to test our character, to see if there is any evil way in us? These are questions that God has brought to my mind on several occasion that would cause me to do some serious self-reflection on my character. As it is written, "Examine yourselves as to whether you are in the faith. Test yourselves. Do you not know yourselves that Jesus Christ is in you? – unless indeed you are disqualified" (2 Corinthians 13:5).

I decided to pray two specific prayers to invite God to reveal to me sins in my heart that I may not aware of so that I may confess my them, repent, and ask for more of Him in my life and less and less of me. As John the Baptist rightly said, "He must increase, but I must decrease" (John 3:30). I prayed, "Search me, O God, and know my heart; try me, and know my thoughts; and see if there be any wicked way in me, and lead me in the way everlasting" (Psalm 139:23, 24). Then I asked God to anoint my hearing so I may hear the words coming out of my mouth, Just like the Bible says, "Ask and it will be given unto you" (Matthew 7:7).

Soon after praying these prayers, God began a deeper work in my heart. I would hear myself make a sarcastic remark or expressed myself in a un-Christ like way. This caused me to ask for discernment that I might understand and identify the root of that sin in my heart. For example, if we find ourselves quick to blame others or become unapproachable or defensive when corrected or criticized, that would be the result of pride. Therefore, pride would be the sin to be confessed of as this is the root, these behaviors and attitudes are just branches. Another example would be if you see someone in need and did not help when it was in your means to do so and later being convicted, we are not to say we are sorry for not giving, but ask for forgiveness for the selfishness of our heart that withheld the act of kindness. Selfishness is the root of the sin and unkindness stemming out from this being the branch. When doing this we are getting to the root of the sin in our lives.

Now I must confess, it has not been easy for me to continue to pray these prayers. I will never forget the first year of my marriage, and my son's teenage years. I sure did discover a lot about myself that I did not like. Many times I have been broken hearted as the Lord has revealed to me just how un-Christ like I am. It hurts knowing that I have wounded Him afresh, and grieved Him as well.

It is also became clear to me that as Christians we are not to lie, nor let corrupt words come out of our mouth. Corrupt communication does not simply refer to something vile and vulgar. I believe this refers also to any communication that will conceal from the mind the view of Christ and blot out from the soul true sympathy and love. We are also counseled to put away all bitterness, wrath, anger, loud quarreling, and evil speaking. We are not to be fornicators, or commit acts of uncleanness, nor be covetous. There should be no foolish talking, nor coarse jesting. We are not just to talk about Christ but reflect His character always. However, over the years I would learn that this does not happen overnight, but by His grace we are by faith to daily surrender to the principles of His Word and allow Jesus to live out His life in us.

One time, God revealed to me just how I had been deceived by Satan in this area of my life. How that often I would say something that was not true and then just say, *"Not really,"* or *"Just kidding".* Jesus made it clear to me that we speak either the truth or a lie. Although I was joking, in reality I was telling a lie. I found myself doing this often, and by my example, my son was picking up this same behavior. One day he called me when he got home from school and said to me that someone had broken into the house and took our T.V and computer. As I began inquiring on how they got in he said to me, *"Not really."* I was a little upset by this, but who was to blame? He learned it from me. I remembered that the Word of God says that as Christians, we are to put these things away. (See Ephesians 4:24; 5:4) Does that mean that God does not want us to laugh? No. I have found that God our Father has a great sense of humor. Let me share this with you.

One day, I was running late and I had to drop off my son at school and go to a job site. We both hurriedly got in the truck, dropped him off and was about half way to work when I looked down and noticed I still had my bedroom slippers on. I just laughed and said to God, "That's a good one." Later on that evening, when I told my son what happened, he had a good laugh too. My heavenly Father was just letting me know that there are enough silly things that we can laugh at without resorting to lies and deceptions.

If we expect to live in the kingdom of heaven, shouldn't our lives reflect the principles of that kingdom right now? After all, if we still wear shoes on our feet in the kingdom of heaven, do you think that we would say to someone "your shoelace is untied" and when they look down you just say, "Just kidding"? But is it the truth or a lie? I encourage you, my friend, to ask God to anoint your hearing and count how many times in a week you say, "Just kidding," "Not really" or "Just messing" or other similar phrase. The point is, as Christians, our conversation is to be different from that of the world. (See 1 Peter 3:10-12)

Have you ever worked with someone or lived next door to a person who just get on your nerves? Often, you think to yourself that unless you get away from this person, you are going to go nuts. They try your patience day after day, and often you find yourself not responding in a Christ-like manner toward them, or talking about them instead of praying for them. Then one day you may go to work or come home to find out that they have moved on. You feel at peace and think to yourself, *what a relief!* Then you find out that the new coworker or neighbor, for some strange reason, acts just like the last person. You might cry out to God like I have and say, *Why me?*

What I have come to learn is Jesus desires to manifest through us a love for all people. That's why He said, "A new commandment I give to you, that you love one another; as I have loved you, that you also love one another. By this all will know that you are My disciples, if you have love for one another." (John 13:34, 35) We can also gather from 1 Corinthians 13:4-7 what love is like. *(I want to encourage you to read verses 4-7 and insert your name everywhere it says "love is" or "is not" and read it back to yourself. It really speaks to me every time I do this.)* This type of love not only applies to our loved ones and our brothers and sisters in the faith, but to all that disagree, ridicule, criticize, and hate us, perhaps showing themselves as our enemies. Jesus made that clear in Luke 6:27-36 and Matthew 5:43-48. "And just as you want men to do to you, you also do to them likewise. But if you love those who love you, what credit is that to you? For even sinners love those who love them. And if you do good to those who do good to you, what credit is that to you? For even sinners do the same" (Luke 6:31-33). I would say this is one of the hardest lessons for me as a Christian to learn, especially in the home for it is here that we often meet the bitterest assaults.

I am also learning to be watchful and prayerful over even the small decisions that I make in life. As I am learning from the Word of God that often it is in the small decisions that we make that human destiny hangs. Such as with Adam and Eve (Genesis 3: 1-7), Israel in the wilderness (Numbers 13:17-14:39.) Samson growing up (Judges 14:1-15:6), Nadab and Abihu (Leviticus 10: 1-11), etc. Their choices not only affected themselves, but also their families, friends and countless others. Choices they made, that perhaps seemed small in their eyes at the time, but had huge and unexpected consequences. And so it is written, "a wise man will hear and increase learning, and a man of understanding will attain wise counsel" (Proverbs 1: 5-6).

In Jeremiah chapter 18, the Lord tells Jeremiah to arise and go down to the potter's house. He there observed the potter making a vessel out of clay, and it was ruined in his hands. So he made it into another vessel and was happy with it. Then the word of the Lord came to Jeremiah saying, "house of Israel, can I not do with you as this potter? Look, as the clay is in the potter's hand, so are you in My hand" (See Jeremiah 18:1-6.) Our Father in Heaven is the Master Worker. He lifts us up out of a horrible pit of sin just as the potter digs up the clay. He then tears it apart and presses it together. He wets it then dries it. Then he lets it lie for a while without touching it. When the potter sees that the clay is perfectly pliable, He continues the work of making of it a vessel. He forms it into shape and on the wheel trims and polishes it. He dries it in the sun and bakes it in the oven (I think that it is during these times I was "kicking and screaming" the most). Yes, we may feel like the clay being "pressed" in the potter's hands. Oh, how compassionate our Father is with us, so longsuffering day by day, wetting us with His grace and giving us time to learn in the school of Christ and absorb His character. Our character is shaped and molded in His precious hands.

Some of these times of refining have been very painful but I know that it is for my good. So the Master worker desires to mold and fashion us, just as the clay is in the hands of the potter, so are we to be in His hands. We are not to try to do the work of the potter. Our part is to yield ourselves to be molded by the Holy Spirit through the Word of God.

There are many people in the Bible that God raised up to be of encouragement to us today. Hebrews chapter eleven mentions many of them that surrender to the molding hands of God becoming vessels of honor, revealing His attributes in the face of great evil and apostasy. The greatest encouragement I have received has been through the study of the life of Christ. I could see that He submitted His humanity to the perfect will of His Father. (See John 6:38, 15:10, 17:4, 6; Luke 22:42,) In return, the Father imparted to His Son all that was necessary for Him to resist all temptation having complete victory over Satan and death. (See Matthew 3:16, 4:11; Luke 22:43, John 17:22.)

Keep in mind when we start our journey with Jesus and continue to grow in the grace and knowledge of Him we are constantly going to be learning not only things about Him but about ourselves. Do not get discouraged, but trust and believe in what Jesus can do for you. Just take it one day at a time. One thing we should never forget is how God has led us in the past. Whatever trial we may face today, or whatever the Lord reveals to us that has to change in our life to walk in harmony with Him, know that His grace and strength will be sufficient to see us through.

Throughout many of my experiences God has given me a clear picture of the old man versus the new man that He was forming within me. He revealed to me my inability to gain victory in my own strength and the importance of surrender to the influence of the Holy Spirit. I have been learning to die to self and let Jesus live out His life in me. I believe this is what Paul meant when he said, "I die daily," and "I have been crucified with Christ; it is no longer I who live, but Christ lives in me" (1 Corinthians 15:31; Galatians 2:20).

Dying to self will certainly be one of the biggest battles we will ever fight. I come to realize that as I have consecrated myself to God, that in character I am to reveal Christ to the world. The self-sacrifice, the sympathy, the love manifested in the life of Christ is to reappear in my life as a Christian. To carry our cross as Jesus has called us is to deny our natural inclination to do wrong and resist the sinful passions of the flesh. It is to practice Christian courtesy even when it is inconvenient to do so. It is to surrender our fight for survival to Him Who is able to provide for our every need. Pride and selfishness must be submitted to the will of God if we are ever to have complete victory over our sinful character traits.

Whether people are obnoxious, arrogant, just outright annoying, or act as an enemy towards us, Jesus taught me that I am to cultivate patience, kindness, and sympathy. Showing them mercy as He has been merciful to me, forgiving as He has been forgiving to me, lest bitterness and resentment rise up in my heart and I be overcome and snared by Satan. Regardless of how someone may treat me, their words and actions are not to dictate my reaction. Although Satan is not permitted to read our thoughts, he is a keen observer, and he marks the words that we use and actions we display when responding to temptation. It is during these situations I am to form a new pattern of behavior, that they may see Christ. If I would labor to repress sinful thoughts and feelings suggested by Satan and through the power of the Holy Spirit give them no expression in words or actions, then people would see the power of the gospel in my life. I am not to say, "The devil made me do it," or, "You pushed my buttons." As a Christian, I realize I should never justify a wrong response because of the way someone has treated me. I make the choice in the end. "For though we walk in the flesh, we do not war after the flesh; (For the weapon of our war-fare are not carnal. But mighty through God to the pulling down of strongholds) Casting down imaginations and every high thing that exalts itself against the knowledge of God, and bringing into captivity every thought to the obedience of Christ; (See 2 Corinthians 10:5).

Sin starts in the mind, and it is here that the battle takes place. As thoughts arise in my mind I am learning to immediately compare that to my knowledge of God's loving character. I ask myself the question, "is this of God or of Satan"? Then if I realize it is of the enemy I would recall the word of God that lifts up in my mind the knowledge of God's goodness and faithfulness and summit to those principles, casting down every imagination and every high thing that exalts itself against the knowledge of God, resisting the devil, causing him to flee. And although he returns many of times to try me again I realize it is a war that I am in, and the Word of God is my defense and shield so I would continue to turn to God and ask for His grace that He has promise would always be sufficient. (See 2 Corinthians 12:9.)

I hope that after reading my story you will see that being a Christian is far from boring. There has been no greater excitement for me than to experience the grace of God in my life and see His power working on my behalf and on behalf of those that my family and I have prayed for and ministered to. In addition, the blessings that He has bestowed upon me are immeasurable, and the one I wait for in the future, by His grace, I shall obtain.

I appeal to you, "Seek ye the Lord while He may be found, call ye upon Him while He is near: Let the wicked forsake his way, and the unrighteous man his thoughts: and let him return unto the Lord, and He will have mercy upon him; and to our God for he will abundantly pardon" (Isaiah 55:6, 7). For "the Lord is righteous in all His ways, gracious in all His works. The Lord is near to all who call upon Him in truth. He will fulfill the desire of those who fear Him; he also will hear their cry and save them. The Lord preserves all who love Him, but all the wicked He will destroy" (Psalm 145:17-20).

The day of my deliverance came and a choice was made. When I sat in darkness, the Lord became a light unto me, and He brought me forth to the light and I beheld His righteousness. Whatever situation you may find yourself in, embrace this promise that God has made to all: "He will regard the prayer of the destitute, and not despise their prayer. For He hath looked down from the height of His sanctuary; from heaven the Lord viewed the earth. To hear the groaning of the prisoner; to release those appointed to death" (Psalm 102:17, 19). For "the wages of sin is death, but the gift of God is eternal life through Christ Jesus our Lord" (Romans 6:23). Therefore, our God and Creator tells us, "Look to Me, and be saved, all you ends of the earth! For I am God, and there is *no other"* (Isaiah 45:22 emphasis mine). "For God sent not His Son into the world to condemn you; But that you through Him might be saved" (John 3:17).

Christ never forces His presence upon anyone. We must ask to receive, acknowledging our need, and He promised He would not leave us or forsake us. Jesus will gladly enter the humblest home and cheer the lowliest heart. However, if we are too proud and indifferent to think of Him or ask Him to come into our hearts and abide with us, He just passes on. This is why many will meet with great loss.

Nevertheless, we need not be afraid. For the promise is made to you, "I know the thoughts that I think towards you, says the Lord, thoughts of peace, and not of evil, to give you a future and a hope" (Jeremiah 29:11). Angels of heaven are going from place to place throughout the earth, seeking to comfort those in sorrow and despair, to protect those in danger, to win the hearts of men, women, and children to Christ. No one is neglected or passed by, for God is no respecter of person.

Know that Jesus Christ is willing to accept you right where you are, with all your wants, imperfections, and weaknesses. He offers forgiveness and cleansing of your sins and invites you to take His yoke and learn of Him. For it is His desire to impart peace and rest to all that come unto Him for the bread of life. He requires us only to perform those duties that will fill our lives with blessings of which the disobedient can never experience. I will say that the greatest joy one could ever experience is to have Christ formed within, "the hope of glory." My friend, "Eye has not seen, nor ear heard, nor have entered in to the heart of man the things which God has prepared for those who love Him" (1 Corinthians 2: 9).

Chapter 20

No Middle Ground

"What fellowship has righteousness with lawlessness? And what communion has light with darkness? ... Therefore, "Come out from among them and be separate, says the Lord. Do not touch what is unclean, and I will receive you." 2 Corinthians 6:14, 17

One day I was having a devotional with my son, who's sixteen at that time, about being careful with our associations. Afterwards, we went out back to clear some trees so that later we could plant a garden. I came across a tree that was dead. I noticed that there was a wild root that grew out of the ground and wrapped itself around the tree, growing up the base of the tree and into the top branches. I think you might know what I am talking about. Have you ever tried to pull one of these vines out of the branches? It is as if you will have to pull the tree down before it comes out. Since the tree is already dead I decided to cut it down and as I was cutting it up in sections to burn, I came across a part of it that was quite amazing to me. The wild vine, slowly over time, wrapped its way completely around this part of the tree and embedded itself into the branch and that they be-

came one. The sad part of it was that the tree eventually died but the wild vine continued to live. I called my son over and showed it to him. We marveled at the goodness of God to give us such an illustration from nature and the spiritual application is so clear and important that we cannot afford to miss it.

My friend, as Christians we are like a tree planted by the Lord (See Psalms 1:3.) It is Him who nourishes us and it's His desire that we become grounded in His word and grow up in Him. But the enemy is also at work. Satan wants to entangle us with the things of this world to "choke the good seed" (Seem Matthew 13: 3-8.) He is seeking to desensitize our thoughts towards sin so that it becomes the norm. This made me realize the importance of separating myself from everything that promotes Satan's character. Jesus wants us to separate ourselves from constant contact with sin, lest we lose the sense of its exceeding sinfulness. Jesus is inviting us to abide in Him that His fruit will be seen and our joy may be full (See John 15:1-11.) He said, "Do not be partakers with them. For you were once in darkness, but now you are light in the Lord. Walk as children of light (for the fruit of the Spirit is in all goodness, righteousness, and truth), finding out what is acceptable to the Lord. And have no fellowship with the unfruitful works of darkness, but rather expose them. For it is shameful even to speak of those things which are done by them in secret (Ephesians 5:7-12). But the question that comes to mind is, what are Satan's tools or devices that he uses to entangle us?

Satan has his signature on much of the media today. The TV, internet, video games, books and magazines are filled with violence and immorality. Much of it endorses the character and attributes of Satan. Do not be deceived, Satan often finds a powerful agency for evil in which he may work through one human mind to exert a bewitching influence upon another human mind. This influence is so seductive that the person who is being molded by it is often unconscious of its power. Remember, the enemy is a master worker of deception and if God's people are not constantly led by the Holy Spirit of God, submitting to His Word/abiding in Him, they will be overcome by Satan and led down the path of destruction.

You may be saying to yourself right now, "You don't know what you're talking about, these things don't affect me." Perhaps you are just not conscious of it. So I ask, "how many times have you watched something or played a video game and started using the same catch phrases, speaking with the same tone of voice, demonstrating the same attitude in which you express yourself, or using the same mannerisms/body language? How many times have demonstrated a behavior that reflected the character of the actor that you have just watched?" Every time I have asked people these questions I always get the same response, "yes I have done that." Then I ask, "what just happened? You were not talking or acting like that the day before or even an hour ago." It is a direct fulfillment of these Bible principles.

"Know ye not, that to whom ye yield yourselves servants to obey, his servants ye are to whom ye obey; whether of sin unto death, or of obedience unto righteousness?" (Romans 6:16).

"Do not be deceived, God is not mocked; for whatever a man sows, that he will also reap. For he who sows to the flesh will of the flesh reap corruption, but he who sows to the Spirit will of the Spirit reap everlasting life" (Galatians 6:7, 8).

"For by whom a person is overcome, by him also he is brought into bondage" (2 Peter 2:19).

The word of God is so powerful and what I find so amazing is that rather a person believes in God and what is stated in His word or not, it does not stop the principles of His word from being effecting the life. Satan know this, and he especially know the power of this next verse.

"But we all with unveiled face, beholding as in a mirror the glory of the Lord, are being transformed into the same image from glory to glory, just as by the Spirit of the Lord" (2 Corinthians 3:18).

I have watched a little child view a cartoon and immediately afterwards go over to their sibling or friend and pull the same trick on them or treat them the same way they have just observed in the cartoon or movie. Again they were not acting like that five minutes ago. Satan know that if he can get us to behold his character instead of the glory of the Lord, we will be transformed into the same image as that of himself. One only needs to look around and we can see all how true this is. As we yield our mind to the characteristics of Satan we have no power in of ourselves to resist his influence and therefore we become his servants, behaving as he would have it. If we yield our minds unto Christ we shall show ourselves to be His children, worshiping Him in Spirit and truth. Thus by beholding Him we shall be changed into His image, reflecting His character, Jesus living out His life in us and we giving heed to His word we become one. Sowing to the Spirit we shall reap everlasting life.

Satan is like a master magician that captivates his subject with illusions, allowing them to see and hear only what he desires, linking his mind to the human mind so that his thoughts become theirs. Jesus pointed out that before His coming that it will be as the days of Noah. We can go back to Genesis 6:5 to understand what it was like in Noah's day. "And God saw that the wickedness of man was great in the earth, and that every *imagination of the thoughts of his heart* was only evil continually" (KJV, emphasis added). I like to take note of the word *imagination,* which means "the act or power of forming mental images of what is not present" (Webster's New World Dictionary, p.316).

Just before the flood, Satan succeeded in manifesting his mind to humanity. The passage does not say that everyone was physically committing acts of evil and wickedness. It says that the imagination of their thinking was evil continually. Satan had succeeded in diverting the mind from meditating upon thoughts of God, His character, and the plan of salvation. He had formed mental images of his character in the minds of those that yielded to him by beholding evil. So long as Satan has his influence upon the mind you are his slave. *"For as he thinks in his heart, so is he" (Proverbs 23:7).* This verse clearly indicates that your thoughts will be revealed in your character, "for every tree is known by its fruit" (See Matthew 7:15-20 and Galatians 5:19-24).

Satan's secret weapon is sorcery. Revelation 18:23 says, "For by your sorceries were *all nations deceived.*" Sorcery is witchcraft and witchcraft is anything that teaches us to rebel against the expressed will of God and His Commandments. In 1 Samuel chapter 15 you can read the story about King Saul. He was commanded by God to do something, yet he only obeyed part of the command. He went forth to do God's command but did not carry it out according to God's direction. When the prophet Samuel came to King Saul, he sought to make excuses for his rejection of God's word, and in verse 23 it is made clear to Saul and to all of us today that *rebellion is as the sin of witchcraft*. In addition, in verse 26 the prophet Samuel tells King Saul, "For you have rejected the Word of the Lord, and the Lord has rejected you from being king over Israel." Here and throughout the Bible it is revealed that God will not honor nor walk with those who reject His Word. "Can two walk together, unless they are agreed?" (Amos 3:3). Moreover, Jesus said, "For whoever is ashamed of Me and *My words*, of him the Son of Man will be ashamed when He comes in His own glory, and in His Father's and of the holy angels" (Luke 9:26).

Another illustration comes to mind. I want to leave you with a word picture that hopefully you will always remember. When you travel, or if you are reading this from a prison cell, when you go to the bathroom do you just sit down on the toilet? I would venture to guess that everyone will answer, NO! So why is it that we wipe off the seat, or place one of those fancy disposable seat covers or toilet paper down on the seat before we sit down? Why do we make such effort to keep germs off our backside and yet allow every type of impurity, violence, and all kinds of evil to come into our minds? Our minds are the very place in which we as professed Christians invite Jesus to reign. You may be laughing right now, but so is Satan. He knows that as long as you are beholding his character traits and thinking upon his suggestions, you are his subject. And when Jesus comes to destroy sin all those that are associated with it will be destroyed as well. The Lord pleads with us, "As I live, says the Lord God, I have no pleasure in the death of the wicked, but that the wicked turn form his way and live. Turn, turn for your evil ways! For why should you die, O house of Israel?" (Ezekiel 33:11). I want you to think about this every time you sit down on a toilet.

As Christians we need to ask ourselves, do the things I partake of promote good or evil? Does it strengthens my relationship with Jesus or does it draw me away from Him? Does it endorse the character traits of Satan, such as murder, lying, hatred, adultery, and covetousness? Does it promote witchcraft, immoral living such as fornication and homosexuality, and teach us to rebel against God? Do the things I partake of pass the test of God's Word that "whatsoever things are true, honest, pure, lovely, of good report, virtuous/of moral goodness, or praiseworthy/

giving honor to God we are to think on these things." (See Philippians 4:8.) This is the standard, not what society sets up.

So what is the solution if we find ourselves attracted to and stimulated by the character traits of Satan? The question is asked, "How can a young man cleanse his way? By taking heed according to Your word (see Psalm 119:9). You will have to become a faithful sentinel over your eyes, ears, and all your senses if you would control your mind and prevent vain and corrupt thoughts from staining your soul. The power of His grace/character dwelling in us alone can accomplish this most desirable work. Only Jesus Christ dwelling in us through the Holy Spirit can bring about a change. Jesus said, "Without Me you can do nothing" (John 15:5). And His word goes on to tell us. "Therefore if anyone cleanses himself from the latter, he will be a vessel for honor, sanctified and useful for the Master, prepared for every good work (2 Timothy 2:21). Let us separate ourselves from this unrighteousness and be followers of Jesus Christ and "let everyone who names the name of Christ depart from iniquity" (2 Timothy 2:19).

In the book of Acts chapter 19 I read a story about the people dwelling in Ephesus. Because of certain things that had happened they feared the Lord and many believed the things told to them about God. And because of this, many that believed came, confessed, and showed their deeds. They brought forth those things that had Satan's signature that revealed his character, and burned them.

As the Lord reveals these things to you, I encourage you to burn and destroy them immediately, as the enemy will tempt you to hang on to them a little longer. Don't listen to him; remember he is a deceiver, liar, and murderer. Also know that Satan would seek to convince you to have a yard sale or just donate these items. Satan will whisper in your ear that you should at least try to get some of your money back and that you can use it for good. However, God says, "Love your neighbor as yourself." Don't sell or give away the tools of Satan that would be used to destroy another soul. God is able to give you much more by being obedient to Him.

Satan knows that there will come a day that God will finally destroy him for all the evil he has done. This is very clear in the Bible in

Ezekiel 28 12-19 giving a description of Satan before he rebelled, what his sin was and how God shall destroy him one day and he will never be again. Therefore, he has set out to deceive as many as possible into serving him so they too will receive the same punishment that he will.

Going back to the tree with a vine wrapped around it, I then pointed to my son to look at where the wild vine started coming out of the ground. It was a little over a foot away. Here, our wonderful Lord had another lesson for us to learn. Don't see how close you can get to the edge of a cliff without falling over. We are prone to think that we can just walk along the edge of apparent evil and not be affected by it. However, just like the tree was near the wild vine, it just came over and attached itself to it because it was close enough. So shall all that is of Satan's character become a part of our life if we choose to behold his influence.

Do not delay, for you have heard His voice and today is the day of salvation. I do not know what greater appeal to make to you, my friend. Be faithful and do what is right. As I have given heed to this counsel and warning, my relationship with Jesus Christ and the Father has grown greatly. Truly wisdom and knowledge of His Word have been the strength of my salvation; and the fear of the Lord has been my treasure. Let not the enemy destroy your witness. "Choose you this day whom you will serve". "If then you were raised with Christ, seek those things which are above where Christ is, sitting at the right hand of God. Set your mind on things above, not on things of the earth. For you died, and your life is hidden with Christ in God" (Colossians 3:1-3). Therefore, let us set no worthless thing before our eyes or allow it come into our hearing (See Psalm 101:3.)

We are not to be partakers or have fellowship with them, but rather expose them. The Bible teaches that it is God's will that we "abstain from every form of evil" (1 Thessalonians 5:22) and that we are to "Fear God and give glory to Him, for the hour of His judgment has come: and worship Him who has made heaven and earth, the sea and springs of water" (Revelation 14:6). In addition we are to "hate evil, pride, arrogance and the evil way. (See Proverbs 8:13.) Moreover, we are counseled by the Word, "Do not be unequally yoked together with unbelievers. For what fellowship has righteousness with lawlessness? And what communion has light with darkness? "Come out from among them and be separate, says the Lord. Do not touch what is unclean. And I will receive you." "I will be a Father to you, and you shall be My sons and daughters, says the Lord Almighty" (2 Corinthians 6:14, 17-18).

Appendix A

Looking at the Evidences

Have you ever lied or been lied to before? I have, and throughout my life I bought into the lies of Satan about the character of God; that He was severe, angry, unforgiving and controlling. I have always listened to what others had to say, and went on living my life as if this was all I would ever have. You have just read what the result of this was, a selfish, prideful life that resulted in discouragement, emptiness, sorrow and pain. I have two questions to ask you that I have started to ask people I run into daily. *"Have you heard people say that if you don't serve God, He is going to burn you in hell forever?"* And "Do you think God is trying to control your life, because He has asked you to live by the Ten Commandments". Ninety percent of the time or more the answers come back as "yes." With what I have already shared with you to this point, I would like to add just another thing to encourage you. I encourage you to search out for yourself what the Bible has to say on these and other questions concerning the true nature and character of God.

As I have continued reading the Bible and from my personal experience, I can see that there is an ongoing war over us, and our final fate. A war greater than any war ever fought between nations here on earth. This one involves everyone now living and all those who have ever lived before us. Some would call it the Great Controversy, between good and evil. Although there may be Christians, Muslims, Jews and perhaps other religions, that may be aware of this fact, I wonder how many understand just how this war started, where it all began and when or how it will end.

The Bible tells us that war broke out in heaven long before wars took place on earth (See Revelation12:7). We need to realize that the opposite of war is peace. God is love and where there is love there is peace; however, peace is only maintained where there is trust. I am convinced that our Creator values nothing higher, than our freedom to choose. Therefore, when He created other beings, in heaven and on this earth, He created them with a free will, a right to choose. What is the choice over? I believe it is over the question, will we trust Him, who created us and loves us and always has our best interest in mind. Will we choose to trust Him or not? For without having trust in Him and who He is, there can be no peace and without peace there can be no unity, and without unity, chaos which leads to war.

Our loving Creator would not have us to be ignorant over what is truly taking place and through His Word He reveals to us the whole story with enough evidence that all may know the truth and make an intelligent choice. As I have reviewed the description in the Bible concerning Satan before he was cast out of heaven, I begin to understand what the great controversy, this war, was all about.

The Beginning

In the book of Ezekiel chapter 28:12-15 God's Word tells us that he, Lucifer, (Light bearer) was the seal of perfection, full of wisdom and perfect in beauty that he was the anointed cherub, highly honored who dwelt continually in the presence of God. He was perfect until iniquity was found in him. Verse 18 says, "You defiled your sanctuaries by the multitude of your iniquities, by the iniquity of your trading" I asked myself "what was he trading?" or as other versions say trafficking? Bible reveals in Isaiah 14:12-14, that Satan coveted the worship that was due to God alone. However in order to secure this worship to himself he would have to convince the other created beings that God was not trustworthy, that His law was unfair, and that He was seeking to keep them from reaching a higher quality of life. It was seen that he hated God's law and all those that keep it (See Revelation 12:17.) So where once there was perfect peace and harmony Lucifer began to sow discord, and discontent. One could only imagine how you would convince someone that lived in a perfect environment that it had now become corrupted. Where was the evidence? Moreover, how could this happen? I read in John 8:44 that Jesus said that Satan was the "father of lies". It was then that I realized just what he was trafficking in, lies. Lies about God's character. Lies about the law of God that governed His government. The law of love, in which God reveals to us the meaning of love in the Ten Commandments. I believe the lies went something like this: We don't need the law of God to tell us how we are to love. We can do this on our own without Him telling us how to do it. Why do I think this was the lie? Because I am still hearing it today. Satan's smooth, cunning tongue convinced one third of the angelic hosts in heaven to side with him in open rebellion against God and His law.

Lucifer pushed his agenda to the point of causing a rebellion in heaven as other angels yielded their minds to his reasoning. Even with the evidence of the love of God before them, these created beings joined Lucifer in his cause. Therefore we have what the Bible calls "the mystery of lawlessness/iniquity" (See 2 Thessalonians 2:7.) Lucifer coveted the worship and reverence that belonged to God alone and was willing to cause war if necessary to get his way. Like a little child that throws a tantrum because he cannot have his way, this created being brought woe and ruin upon a perfect universe for his own personal gain.

God does not make mere claims as to His true nature as Lucifer continues to do. Instead, he prepared to demonstrate before the entire universe that He is love and values nothing higher than the freedom of all His created beings. The Bible tells us what happened next. "War broke out in heaven. Michael and His angels fought against the dragon, and the dragon and his angels fought, but did not prevail, nor was a place found for them in heaven any longer. So the great dragon was cast out, that serpent of old, called the devil and Satan, *who deceives the whole world*; he was cast to the earth, and his angels were cast out with him. Then I heard a loud voice saying in heaven, now salvation, and strength, and the kingdom of our God, and the power of His Christ have come, for the accuser of our brethren, who accused them before our God day and night, has been cast down…. Woe to the inhabitants of the earth and of the sea! For the devil is come down unto you, having great wrath, because he knows that he hath but a short time" (Revelation 12:7-10, 12). Sin separates us from God (See Isaiah 59:2,) therefore, God gave them up to the choices they had made, and now all those that partook of the rebellion were cast out of heaven. No longer able to sow discord in heaven, Satan now set out to cause woe and misery upon God's new creation.

God's Plan

God created man to bear His image; he was created to reflect the perfect character of God. He came forth from His Maker in harmony with His law of love, with a mind capable of comprehending divine things. Adam and Eve were created with noble traits of character, with no preconceived notion toward evil. Their affections towards God were pure with no reason to distrust or doubt His love. Although our parents were created innocent and holy they were still given the freedom of choice. They could continue to give their affections to God through obedience to the divine requirements in peace, or chose to reject God's ideal of government. I believe it was God Himself who personally informed Adam and Eve in the Garden concerning the nature of Satan's rebellion in heaven, his ability to deceive those who choose to listen to his lies and the death that would be the result if they choose to follow him.

God never intended for us to know evil. He placed our parents in a beautiful garden and told them they could eat of every tree in the garden except one, that was the tree of the knowledge of good and evil (See Genesis 2:16, 17.) God was wise in the counsel that He had given them. He was not trying to withhold from them anything that was for their best interest to have. In His wisdom He was setting a boundary of protection for them. Satan could only have access to them at the tree of the knowledge of good and evil. As long as they stayed away from it they were showing their loyalty to their Creator and Friend and would be safe.

We cannot serve two masters, we either serve God through a trusting (faithful), obedient relationship with Him, or we serve His enemy Satan by yielding our mind to his reasoning, his lies and his control. If God placed you in a room and told you that you could walk through any door and find joy and happiness except one, would you not ask the question what is behind that one door? I am sure our first parents inquired concerning what would happen to them if they were to eat of the tree. Complete separation from His life giving glory and their death. It was already on record that to distrust God and reject His love would bring about separation. Sin is like a poison it may not kill us right away but once set in motion without a remedy the end result will always be death.

As I continued to read the record of the sad story that took place in Genesis chapter 3, Eve apparently wandered from her husbands' side and found herself gazing upon the tree of the Knowledge of Good and Evil. Being warned of the fallen foe Eve did not take into consideration that he could approach her in disguise, as it is this day with many of us. We are unaware of the many disguises that Satan uses to arrest our attention and delight the eye of the beholder. He took the form of a serpent to excite her curiosity and once she was looking upon the beautiful forbidden fruit he began to reason with her. And he said to the woman, "Has God indeed said, you shall not eat of every tree of the garden?" Instead of fleeing, she stayed to listen. Perhaps she did not think that the fascinating serpent she saw could be the fallen foe. And then she answered, "We may eat the fruit of the trees of the garden; but of the fruit of the tree which is in the midst of the garden, God has said, you shall not eat it, nor shall you touch it, lest you die." And the serpent said to the woman, "you will not surely die. For God knows that in the day you eat of it your eyes will be opened and you will be like God, knowing good and evil." So when the woman saw that the tree was good for food, that it was pleasant to the eyes, and a tree desirable to make one wise, she took of its fruit and ate. She also gave to her husband and he ate. Then the eyes of both of them were opened, and they knew that they were naked; they sewed fig leaves together and made themselves coverings (See Genesis 3:1-7.) Please take note of how Satan gains access to the mind through the five senses. She decided to look with curiosity upon what was forbidden, she was willing to listen to Satan, she touched what was forbidden, smelled and tasted to her ruin. As with Eve, I could clearly see how I too could be overcome if I neglected the clear counsel of God. Because Eve was willing to enter into a conversation with Satan. Satan was able to begin reasoning with her, insinuating that the divine warning was just to intimidate them and would not actually be fulfilled. Satan convinced Eve that God had been seeking to prevent them from reaching a higher development of life and finding greater happiness.

In my life He has also whispered those same lies, that I can live a lawless life, transgressing the Commandments of God and still live forever. When the Word of God clearly says, "The soul who sins shall die" (Ezekiel 18:4). As I read His Word, immortally is only granted to those who trust (have Faith in) Him through obedience to His Commandments. (See Revelation 22:14.) The enemy says that if you walk in opposition to the principles of love; to do what you like, this will bring you peace, joy and pleasure. God's Word tells me however, "Great peace have they which love My law" and "I will show you the path of life; In My presence is fullness of joy; at My right hand are pleasures forevermore" (Psalms 119:165; 16:11). This has been the way he has worked for over 6,000 years. Satan mixes lies with truth as he continues to do in order to deceive us. So the sin of our first parents was not that they believed a lie, their sin was that they did not believe the truth that God had revealed to them.

The Effect

Now that they had eaten of the poison of sin it immediately began to affect them. Satan deceived them into sin and now they found themselves naked and afraid of God, their Creator and Friend. What were they afraid of? The fear of His presence and discovery of their disobedience to His Word, along with the penalty that was to result due to their rebellion. With a sense of guilt and uncertainty of the future they thought to hide themselves from Him who was once their daily delight. Sin will always have the same affect wherever it is given entrance, until a remedy is introduced and received. Oh how God must have cried as He watched them make their choices. I imagine all the hosts of heaven watching to see God's response to this newly created couple who stood afraid and in hiding.

In Genesis 3:8-15, we see a wonderful loving Father longing to save His children and heal them from the damage done by their choices. Not a severe Judge ready to condemn and execute the death penalty. After they had sinned, God came to commune with them, and they attempted to hide from His presences, just like children do today when they do something wrong. However, God knowing what they had done did not leave them to wallow in guilt and shame, but pursued them as His lost children, verse 8.

I can see how the influence of sin immediately affected the lives of Adam and Eve. They no sooner sinned then their nature immediately began to show signs of moral corruption, the poison was making its effect. They had lost their strength to resist evil and had now opened the way for Satan to gain control of them. "For by whom a person is overcome, by him also he is brought into bondage/slavery" (See 2 Peter 2:19.) They now began to reveal the characteristics of the one to whom they had yielded there mind. The spirit of self-justification originated with Satan (the father of lies) and was now being manifested in Adam and Eve. This same spirit has been seen in all the sons and daughter of Adam. Instead of us confessing our sins with humility, we try to shield ourselves by casting blame upon others, upon circumstances, and even upon God.

It is here that I began to see in His Word that God is not just about making claims that He is love, but demonstrates love by how He deals with His wayward children. God choose to be longsuffering and respond in a positive way to a very negative situation. He was slow to anger revealing His complete understanding of the great controversy taking place over their souls. Although they had cast blame upon Him and one another, He showed His great love for them by not repaying evil for evil. Then when speaking to Satan in the hearing of Adam and Eve He promised a Redeemer would come, it would be His only Son, who would pay the price for their sin, and place hatred in their heart towards sin, but not the sinner.

The angels in heaven as well as our first parents had never heard a lie spoken to them before. However we, Adam's descendants, have been hearing lies our whole life. The majority of the time we take it hook, line and sinker as some would say. They, both those in heaven and on earth had all the evidence of God's love before their eyes yet they choose to allow Lucifer (now called Satan, the accuser) to reason with them long enough that they believed the lie when they had the evidence right before them of the truth. That is scary! It is now clear to me that we are dealing with a very highly intelligent supernatural created being. Smarter than you or I will ever be. It also showed to me the importance of each one of us personally searching the scriptures for ourselves to find out what the real truth is. So that we can make an informed choice for ourselves, as to whom we will trust and whom we will serve.

To Restore

From the fall in the garden all the way to the cross at Calvary God has demonstrated His attributes of love towards His wayward children. After delivering Israel from slavery God did not demand that they love Him, He simply told them how they were to show their love to Him and their fellow man and not to continue to behave as they did in the past. Coming out of an idolatrous environment their morals where perverted and they had no understanding of the meaning of love. Therefore, He tells them that the first four of the Ten Commandments were how to show their love to Him and in the last six how they are to love one another (See Exodus 20:1-17.) Now I understand why when Jesus delivered me from being a slave to Satan He pointed me to His perfect Law. As I looked upon the divine law I can see just how out of harmony my life had become to those principles of love. The law pointed me back to my Savior, Jesus Christ, the only One that could heal me and give me the grace to walk in harmony and obedience to the Ten Commandments, the principles of love (See John 1:12 and Acts 5:32). Therefore, I could see my need of Jesus Christ dwelling in me by the Power of the Holy Spirit, for I to abide in Christ and for Christ to abide in me. As I read the history of Israel from their delivery out of Egypt until after the death and resurrection of Christ, I see a Loving Father in pursuit of His wayward children. When they mocked the messengers of God, and despised His words, and misused His prophets, what more could He do? He gave them up to their desires. When God withdraws His protection from us because we reject Him, who is left to take over? Satan. Through the history of Israel, God has shown me that if I reject the only One that can protect me from the power of Satan, I cut myself off from my only source of hope. "To them God willed to make known what are the riches of the glory of this mystery among the Gentiles: which is Christ in you, the hope of glory" (Colossians 1:27).

The goodness of God is revealed throughout the Bible from the very beginning to the very end. "Behold, the Lord's hand is not short-ened, that it cannot save. Nor His ear heavy, that it cannot hear" (Isaiah 59:1). "His mercy endures forever". It is this wondrous love that amazes me every time I read His Word. Now when I read the Bible I ask myself the question. "What does this story tell me about the character of God in view of the great controversy?" In the Gospels, I see that Jesus came to heal, forgive and restore. Also to reflect the proper correct image of His Father's Character, so long misrepresented. When asked by one of His disciples to show them the Father, He replied, "Have I been with you so long, and yet you have not known Me Philip? He who has seen Me has seen the Father; so how can you say, "Show me the Father" (John 14:8, 9). His whole life was a demonstration of the meaning of love in action. In addition, He came to deliver us all from the fear that started in the garden, the fear of death (See Hebrews 2:14, 15.)

My Response

In reviewing the fall of one-third of the host of heaven and of our first parents I noticed some things in common. Both parties **were deceived and thereby rejected the evidence of God's love that was before them.** They **allowed** Satan **to reason with them and welcomed his insinuations of doubt.** Due to this there was a **breakdown of trust** *(faith)* **in their relationship with their Creator and Friend. This led them to doubt His love and reject His wisdom.** And as it was Satan custom he would point to God and blame all this upon Him, saying that His Commandments were hard, that He was severe and not trustworthy.

As for me, I have found that God's Word reveals the true nature of God's character. *God is love* (1 John 4:8) and love does not force itself upon anyone. The law of love is the foundation of the govern-ment of God and the happiness of all created beings depends upon them choosing to live in harmony with the great principles founded in His

Love. God desires all His creatures to love Him and serve Him out of appreciation of His loving character. He takes no pleasure in and will not force obedience from His creation to Himself. Therefore He has given us all the freedom of choice. Upon discovering this throughout the Bible, it is clear to me that any religion that seeks to bring people into subjection through fear or persecute people into submission to its authority is of Satan.

Through my own experience I could see that God is longsuffering, and goes to great lengths to reveal Himself to us. It is here that many misunderstand God when great evils are committed and justice is not render immediately. People question God, "why?" "If you are love, why is there so much evil and suffering in this world?" I thought to myself "why did He not just destroy Lucifer"? He created him, He could have easily excised his power to destroy, but is that love? However, there is more to this great controversy than just who has more power and authority. It is all about who is telling the truth. The Word of God is clear and it was Jesus, who revealed it by the cross, that love does not destroy those who will not rendered back to Him that love. Instead, God allows us our own choices and in the end we reap what we sow (See 2 Chronicles 30:7; Psalms 81:11, 12; Romans 1:18-31 note verses 24, 26, 28.) Here we can see then that God does not command us to love Him out of fear of our destruction. He leaves us to our choices, either to side with Him and celebrate the victory Jesus gained for us at the cross and follow Him or believe the lies of Satan that in the end leads to our death and destruction. Because we will have rejected the only remedy to sin, Jesus Christ, this is what our final outcome will be. Had our Creator destroyed Lucifer for his rebellion before the angelic hosts, while still in heaven, all would have worshiped Him out of fear. And where there is fear there is no peace or trust/faith. For the Bible say "There is no fear in love; perfect love casts out fear" 1 John 4:18. Seeds of fear in the end will only produce rebellion, this I know from my own experience.

I also had bought into the lies of Satan, not investigating the evidence for myself. My sole purpose for most of my life was to live for what I could get out of this world, a very selfish, self-centered life, subconsciously living in fear of death. I had been a slave to sin (lawlessness), which I now see as "loveless-ness". I know that is not an actual word, but when I think of lawlessness that's what comes to mind, without love, but a selfish love. I then picture Jesus hanging on the cross for my sins and I hear Him asking me ***"will you trust me now?"*** Investigating the evidence for *myself* it has become clear to me there is no need to be afraid of God. He does not command me to love and serve Him or He will punish me in hell fire. Nor is He seeking to dictate and control my life by asking me to love Him and my fellow man by keeping all of His Commandments. He has proven Himself trustworthy and has only asked me to give up habits and turn from behaviors that brought separation between us. In His perfect love He has always had my best interests and good in mind in all His dealings with me. His desire has always been to bring healing to me and restore in me the image of His Son. That I might be able to spend the rest of eternity with Him living in perfect peace, joy and love. Each day I spend with Him makes this more and more a reality. What about you reader, is that your desire as well? If so I would like to encourage you to "Acquaint now yourself with Him, and be at peace: whereby good shall come to you. Receive, I pray, the law from His mouth, and lay up His words in your heart (Job 22:21-22).

Appendix B

The Law of Love

I recall reading a passage one day that really caused me to reflect upon my walk with God. "A good man out of the good treasure of his heart brings forth good; and an evil man out of the evil treasure of his heart brings forth evil. For out of the abundance of the heart his mouth speaks. But why do you call Me 'Lord, Lord,' and not do the things which I say?" (Luke 6:45, 46). I read the fourth and fifth chapters of Ephesians, and the third chapter of Colossians, and saw a standard being laid out for the Christian to walk in. In addition, the fifth and sixth chapter of Romans brings it all home. (Please read all of the above.) For how shall a man live on what he died of? Sin brings death; therefore, how can a Christian live on what he once died to? He that is dead to sin is then freed from its power. For it is the will of God that sin should not have dominion over us. But through His grace we are brought into harmony with His Ten Commandments of love and the principles of His Word.

The Bible tells us that Jesus came to save us from sin. (See Matthew 1:21; John 1:29.) We already know from previous chapters that sin is the transgression of God's Law. There is only one law that

God has spoken, and written on stone, signifying that it can never be changed. (See Exodus 31:18.) So I ask, is it wrong for God to want to save us from sin that separates us from Him? (See Isaiah 59:2.) Is it wrong for Him to ask us to live according to a set of laws that were given to safeguard our happiness? As we read the Ten Commandments in Exodus chapter 20:1-17 it does reveal that these are expressions of the great commandment which is to love God above all and to love one another as God has loved us. Sin has caused us to be selfish, prideful and unloving. So the Ten Commandments were given by God to show us how to love God who created us and how to love our fellow men. These ten principles of love have never been against us or nailed to the cross as I have heard so many pastors and Christians say. You can no more do away with or change this Law than you could do away with God Himself. God changes not (See Malachi 3:6, Hebrews 13:8,) nor does His law, which is the basis of His government. For He has said, "My covenant I will not break, nor alter the word that has gone out of My lips" (Psalm 89:34). The law was not only written with the finger of God, but He also spoke it in the hearing of the people. That is why Jesus also said, "Do not think that I came to destroy the Law or the Prophets. I did not come to destroy but to fulfill" (Matthew 5:17). He came not only to fulfill all that the prophets have spoken of Him but also to demonstrate how we are to abide in His love, through the keeping of His commandments. Jesus says to us, "If you keep My commandments, you will abide in My love, just as I have kept My Father's commandments and abide in His love" (John 15:10). We are incapable of loving others the way God would have us; a self-sacrificing, unselfish love, a love that even embraces our enemies. Jesus asked us to, "Abide in Me, and I in you. As the branch cannot bear fruit of itself, unless it abides in the vine, neither can you, unless you abide in Me. I am the vine, you are the branches. He who abides in Me, and I in him, bears much fruit; for without Me you can do nothing" (John 15:4, 5). Without Jesus Christ dwelling in our hearts, living out His life in us we are unable to access the source of that love. To say that we love God, and yet we break any one of His commandments is to make ourselves liars (See 1John 2:4.) God is love, and he who abides in love abides in God, and God in him (1 John 4:16).

Points to Consider

So I ask you, my friend, is it wrong for God to ask us not to kill? Not to commit adultery, to steal or lie? Is it wrong then that He would ask us not to give our highest affections to any other person or object, but to worship Him supremely and serve Him for our greatest joy? Is it wrong to have no other gods before Him? After all, He did create us and redeemed us through the life of His only begotten Son. We belong to Him twice over. Is it wrong that He would ask us to come and spend time with Him on the day *He has chosen*, the seventh day Sabbath, to celebrate with Him the creation of the world, to rest from all our labors and reflect upon His awesome love and plan of salvation? I could clearly see this is the day of rest established before sin entered the world (See Genesis 2:3.) It will be the same day that all flesh shall come together to worship Him when He recreates the heavens and the earth (See Isaiah 66: 22, 23.) Will we say to God then that, "that is only for the Jews" or "there you go again putting us under the law"? As I have heard so many say. I sure hope not.

As I have asked these questions over and over I have always gotten the same response: NO! Once my brother asked me, if God gives us free choice why did He establish a law that we are to abide by? I asked him rather or not every government of the world had some type of law that they expected their citizens to live by. And are the citizens not given the choice to obey it or not? He said yes, so I asked, is it so strange that God would have a set of laws that He has established for His citizens to abide by? It is the law of love, in which all Ten Commandments are founded. The law points us to Christ (Galatians 3: 24), and Christ points us back to the law as He did with the rich young ruler (Mark 10: 17-27). Throughout His life He taught the spiritual nature of the law, and its far-reaching claims for the law is spiritual (Romans 7:14). He manifested in His life that, love to God and man must dwell in the heart and manage the life and be the spring of every thought and action. He taught us this lesson by example and inviting others to follow Him. In addition, He made it clear that nothing in that law could ever change, even slightly (See Matthew 5:18.) Not only that, but as you look upon the next verses you will discover, as I did, that the law of God is a reflection of His character.

God	*His Law*
God is Spiritual – *John 4:24*	**His law is Spiritual** – *Romans 7:14*
God is Love – *1 John 4:8*	**His law is Love** – *Matthew 22:37-40*
God is Truth – *John 4:6*	**His law is Truth** – *Psalm 119:142*
God is Righteous – *1 Cor. 1:30*	**His law is Righteous** – *Psalm 119:172*
God is Holy – *Isaiah 6:3*	**His law is Holy** – *Romans 7:12*
God is Perfect – *Matthew 5:48*	**His law is Perfect** – *Psalm 19:7*
God stands forever – *James 1:17*	**His law stands forever** – *Ps. 111:7, 8*
God is Good – *Luke 18:19*	**His law is Good** – *Romans 7:12*
God is Just – *Deuteronomy 32:4*	**His law is Just** – *Romans 7:12*
God is Pure – *1 John 3:3*	**His law is Pure** – *Psalm 19:8*
God is Unchangeable – *James. 1:17*	**His law is unchangeable** – *Matt. 5:18*

When I discovered all of these verses I was just amazed. I once read, "By all that He requires of thee, know thou what God Himself must be" (author unknown). This is why God desires to write His law in the hearts and minds of everyone that will believe on Him. (See Hebrews 10:15.) And as I look over the list of character traits contained in His law, it is truly for our best interest, that this will bring life, life more abundant. In addition, God adds a blessing to all those that abide by His law. For example;

"Blessed are those who keep justice, and he who does righteousness at all times" (Psalm 106:3).

"Blessed are the undefiled in the way, who walk in the law of the Lord! Blessed are those who keep His testimonies, who seek Him with the whole heart! They also do no iniquity; they walk in His ways" (Psalm 119:1-3).

"Blessed is the man who listens to Me. ... for whoever finds Me finds life, and obtains favor from the Lord; But he who sins against Me wrongs his own soul; All those who hate Me love death" (Proverbs 8:34-36).

"Blessed are those who hear the word of God and keep it" (Luke 11:28).

This next one is my favorite blessing that I am looking forward to:

"Blessed are they that do His commandments that they may have the right to the tree of life, and may enter through the gates into the city" (Revelation 22:14).

Many people want Jesus to come to put an end to the many evils in the world. They are tired of oppression, hatred, wars, disease, sickness, famine, death, and tired of being a slave to man. What I find interesting is that these are the same reasons why the Jews wanted the Messiah to come when in bondage to Rome. These might seem like good reasons; however, while many lament the results of sin, how few there are that want healing and victory from the damage that sin has caused and the separation from God it has brought about. Sin is a breakdown of trust; it's rebellion against God and the principles of love.

We lament the condition of the world, but what are we doing to bring it all to an end? It will only end when Jesus returns, and we are told to look for and hasten the Lord's coming (See 2 Peter 3:12.) But I believe that unless we come to know God as it is our privilege to know Him, forming that trusting relationship that will set us free from sin we will only contribute to these evils. I realize that some may disagree with me, however the bible tells us that Jesus gave Himself for us, that He might redeem us from all *iniquity*, and *purify* unto Himself a *peculiar people*, zealous of good works (See Titus 3:14.)

So before Jesus returns there will be a group of people that will show to the world that it is possible to live out the biblical principles of love, keeping *all* Ten of the Commandments having victory over all sin being set free by the truth having become mature Christians, thus Christ living out His life in us. I found it to be interesting that in the book of Revelation chapter 13:16, 17 it talks about a people group that will have a mark or the ***name of the beast*** or the number of his name either in their hand or forehead. Then chapter 14:1-5, it talks about a people group that follow the Lamb/Jesus where ever He goes. They have no deceit in their mouth and they have the ***Father's name*** written in their forehead. I chose to have the name of God, His character written in my forehead not Satan and his character. How about you my friend? We must "enter by the narrow gate; for wide is the gate and broad is the way the leads to destruction, and there are many who go in by it. Because narrow is the gate and difficult is the way which leads to life, and there are few who find it" (Matthew 7:13, 14).

Appendix C

Light vs. Darkness

*I*s it a common thing to see a child afraid of the dark? However, it is very odd to see a full-grown person afraid of the light. Jesus is light, and life, so why are we afraid of Him? My friend, if God only wants to save us from sin and bestow blessings upon us why are we afraid of making a full surrender to live up to the light found in His Word? I can think of four reasons.

First, I believe many people, including Christians, don't know or understand God's true character. God is love; He is a Father seeking to guide and protect His children from deception and sin, and if we would prayerfully study our Bibles, allowing the Word of God to interpret itself, I do believe all would come to this conclusion.

Second, I believe people are afraid of God because it requires change. Many think that there are too many sacrifices to make to be a Christian. However, what are we really giving up? Error for truth that will set us free; light for darkness that brings us peace and hope amid confusion and despair; weakness for strength; sin for righteousness; a perishable name for honors that are lasting; and an eternal treasure.

Sure, following Christ could mean broken friendships with worldly relatives and friends, but look at the exchange: our names will be written in the Lamb's book of life as partakers of salvation and joint heirs with Jesus Christ. I can testify that we give up nothing that is worth having, our loving Father would never have us give up anything that was not for our best interest to retain. In all that He asks of us, He has our best interests and well-being in mind.

Third, I believe pride/self-image and fear have been a chain that has bound many, including Christians. People are afraid of what their friends might say if they decide to read the Bible. They are fearful of ridicule and criticism, afraid of rejection of friends and family if they choose to go to church. I can say from experience, that if this is your case, they were never your friends to begin with. Then there are some who if they are convicted by the Word of God would rather believe tradition and reject the Word and grieve the Holy Spirit, fearing man rather than God. Because they find themselves shunned by family, friends, and other church members, forgetting the promise, "Blessed are those who are persecuted for righteousness' sake, for theirs is the kingdom of heaven (Matthew 5:10). If you find yourself in a church like this you might want to ask yourself whether that is the kind of love that God has for us. Although people may reject God, or walk contrary to His law, He does not shun or cast them off, but instead He suffers long with them and continues to woo them by His love. If they still reject Him then He leaves them to their choices, but still loves them, for God is love.

The fourth reason why I believe people do not seek out God is that they are comfortable in their lifestyle and feel no need of His healing, guidance or protection. Although their conscience bearing witness of their sin through conviction of the Holy Spirit they just look around at what others are doing and judge that they are not that bad. They do not compare themselves to the great standard of righteousness in the Law of God. This was one of my problems. Some have what they believe to be all they need in life and are happy, while others consider it to be too great of a sacrifice to give up their sinful living.

The Ministry of Trials

Still others believe that to follow God will only mean trials and hardships in life. I found that trials, tribulations and difficulties can be a benefit to us. As He who alone reads the hearts of men knows my character better than I do (See 1 Chronicles 28:9.) In His providence, He has brought me into different positions and varied circumstances that I may discover in my character the defects that have been concealed from my knowledge.

Jesus said in this world we would have tribulation, but we may have peace in Him because He has overcome the world (See John 16:33.) Jesus will strengthen, encourage and see us through all things. As He did with Joseph when he was a slave and a prisoner (See Genesis chapters 39-41.) As He did with Israel delivering them from slavery through the plagues that fell upon Egypt (See Exodus chapter 5-12.) As with Daniel's three friends delivering them through the fiery furnace (See Daniel 3:1-30.) In addition, our Lord delivered Daniel from the lion's den (See Daniel 6:1-23.) Let us not forget the awesome story of Job. Powerful testimony! Apostle Paul testifies, "You have carefully followed my doctrine, manner of life, purpose, faith, longsuffering, love, perseverance, persecutions, afflictions, which happened to me at Antioch, at Iconium, at Lystra – what persecutions I endured. *And out of them all the Lord delivered me.* Yes, and all who desire to live godly in Christ Jesus will suffer persecution (2 Timothy 3:10-12 emphasis added).

Here is a favorite promise from God, our Loving Father that has encouraged me through times of trials and difficulties. "When you pass through the waters, I will be with you; And through the rivers, they shall not overflow you. When you walk through the fire, you shall not be burned, nor shall the flame scorch you." (Isaiah 43:2). That's why the Apostle Peter was inspired to write to us, "Beloved, do not think it strange concerning the fiery trial which is to try you, as though some strange thing has happened to you; but rejoice to the extent that you partake of Christ's sufferings, that when His glory is revealed, you may be glad with exceeding joy" (1 Peter 4:12, 13).

158 / A Drop of Grace

Often Satan will desire to sift us as wheat as he did with Peter. But let us be encouraged not to give up for Jesus says to you and me today, "I have prayed for you, that your faith should not fail." (See Luke 22:31, 32.) I also keep in mind the love He has set upon me through the promise that He will never leave me nor forsake me (See Hebrews 13:5.) I know that it is not His desire to overwhelm me with guilt, but to restore my character to His likeness. Each time I have asked this the Holy Spirit has revealed something else to me, and as I submitted to the convictions of God, I have noticed a change in my character. Although at times He has had to bring me over the same ground more than once before I would learn my true condition or the lesson He was seeking to teach me.

We should be "growing in the grace and knowledge of our Lord and Savior Jesus Christ" (See 1 Peter 3:18.) The fact that we as children of God are called upon to endure such trials shows that the Lord Jesus sees in us something precious that He desires to develop. This has inspired me to rejoice in all things. As "all things work together for good to those who love God, to those who are the called according to His purpose. For whom He foreknew, He also predestined to be conformed to the image of His Son…" (Romans 8:28, 29). Again, it is only by beholding His life and love for me through His sacrifice that I could do this as well.

The Christian's Assurance

As I know from my own experiences there is no desire for the sinner to please God. Because he only lives to please self he will never experience the sense of God rejoicing over him nor of His approval. He will always live under a sense of conviction, striving with the Holy Spirit until he grieves away the Spirit of God or goes down to the grave. He will not enjoy his worldly living and sinful life without trouble. For says the Lord, "The wicked are like the troubled sea, when it cannot rest, whose waters cast up mire and dirt. There is not peace, says my God, for the wicked" (Isaiah 57:20, 21). Because of guilt from a life of sin, the sinner will experience strong emotional pain, especially embarrassment or shame from their course of actions, and reap internal stress as a result. Many times they will find themselves fearful, troubled, and struggle to have peace of mind. Let it be clear that the sinner is not free from disappointments, perplexity, earthly losses, poverty, and distresses in life. In addition, the sinner often suffers from lingering sickness and disease, yet has no mighty arm to lean upon, no grace to strengthen him, and no comfort or power from God to support him. In his weakness he must lean upon his own strength and the comfort of man. He receives no hope as his days fade away, for he cannot look forward with any pleasure to the day of resurrection. He is tormented with a fearful uncertainty of his future and bears his trials alone. Thus the scripture is fulfilled, "Cursed is the man who trusts in man and makes flesh his strength" (Jeremiah 17:5). He closes his eyes in death and goes down into the grave, suffering remorse, under darkness, bound by Satan, for he served his master and in return receives his wages in full. This is the end of a poor sinner's life of vain pleasure. He will come up from the grave at the end of the world (Matthew 13:39) to give an account of his life and pay the price for his sins. But before he meets with that final destiny he will see that all could have been different had he accepted the gift of God, Jesus Christ, as his Savior and cast off the world to walk with Him. He will confess that God is righteous and deserving of praise. (See Romans 14:11 and Philippians 2:10, 11.) Destruction will be his choice rather than live in the presence of a holy, pure and just God. Heaven would be a torment for him because the principles there would be just the opposite of what he loved in this world. In the end, God destroying the sinner and making an utter end of sin will again show His mercy to those that have rejected His love through the gift of salvation.

The faithful Christian is also subject to sickness and disease, earthly losses, reproaches, disappointments, poverty, and distress. However, amid all these he loves God and knows Him in whom he has trusted. Although he loses all and the whole world is against him, his greatest desire is to do the will of God and bring honor to Him. Nothing is more important to him than to bring joy to the heart of God and a smile to His face, knowing that one day God will rejoice over him with singing for doing those things that are pleasing in His sight (See Zephaniah 3:17.) Amid conflicts, trials, and the changing scenes of this life he knows that God understands it all, for Jesus walked in the shoes of humanity once. He knows that God will bend His ear to hear his cries of sorrow and distress, for he has experienced that the Lord is very pitiful and of tender mercy. He is One who can sympathize with his every weakness and comfort the anguish of his heart. For the Christian, who once was a poor sinner, has answered the call to come to Jesus and find rest. In all his affliction the Christian is comforted by the presence of God and greatly encouraged by His Word. Therefore, although he meets with many afflictions, he has the promise that the Lord will deliver him out of them all, and that God will grant him perfect peace because his mind has stayed upon his Mighty Redeemer. (See Psalm 34:19 and Isaiah 26:3.)

And if he suffers a lingering sickness, before he closes his eyes in death, he can bear it with all cheerfulness for he holds communion with his Maker, and He holds fast to the promises of His Word. Therefore, his countenance is radiant with joy as he contemplates his future on resurrection morning. For he knows that it is only a short rest in the grave before He will hear the voice calling him forth from his dusty bed, giving him victory over death, granting him immortality, never again to know pain, sorrow, or death.

This is the hope of the faithful Christian, and because I have answered the call this is my hope as well. Truly, there has been no greater joy which has ever filled my heart than to walk with God and have the opportunity to reflect the character of Jesus Christ to a dying world. This has been an awesome journey, and each day that passes I can truly say my experience with God grows ever stronger. It is my prayer to walk with God as Enoch walked, that I may perhaps be taken up to heaven like him at the second coming of our Lord and Savior Jesus Christ. For I know that all the signs of His soon coming are being fulfilled before our eyes.

Appendix D

The Power of His Grace

Although I have been told that grace means unmerited favor, I could not understand how God's favor alone could change my heart. After all, I had been on the receiving end of God's unmerited favor for some time, but still failing to gain complete victory over my sins. I recall hearing a story that was to demonstrate the grace of God. It went like this: A policeman pulled over a person for speeding. The person was truly guilty of the crime. However, as the officer was about to write up the ticket, he reconsidered and decided to just give a warning to the driver and letting him go, showing him favor. Now the driver, being grateful for the favor, just drove off slowly and did not speed off down the road. This example of grace I do not believe shows the complete character of God. Granted, grace does mean favor in the Hebrew language. This favor is shown to us by the penalty of our transgression falling up Jesus Christ the Son of God. However, in addition God our Father through Jesus Christ goes further than this, stating, "By grace you have been saved through faith, and that not of yourselves; it is a gift of God" (Ephesians 2:8). This inspired me to look up the meaning of grace in Greek. I got out my Strong's Exhaustive Concordance of the Bible and looked up the word grace, and it made reference to "the divine influence upon the heart, and its reflection in the life." This grace referred to in the New Testament is the power of the gospel. Now, when I put everything together in the Old and New Testaments it becomes clearer. The believer benefits from the favor of God by accepting the loving sacrifice that Jesus Christ has made in their behalf. In addition, by asking for the Holy Spirit (Luke 11:13), the Holy Spirit brings a transforming influence into the life, producing the fruit of the Spirit and giving strength to the believer to live by every word that has proceeded out of the mouth of God. Here as a believer we receive a new heart and a new spirit that was promised by God in Ezekiel 36:25-27. Therefore, we are saved by grace/His character through trusting in Jesus to live out His life in us through the principles of His Word. What a wonderful gift from God. We can never take credit for any obedience to His Word or love shown to others. We can only say, "I have been crucified with Christ; it is no longer I who live, but Christ lives in me ..." (Galatians 2:20). All the glory goes to God. We can see that through the promise "where sin abounded, grace shall abound much more," and when the enemy comes in like a flood to increase sin in a believer's life, the Spirit of the Lord lifts up a standard against him (See Isaiah 59:19.)

Through my experiences and the study of God's Word, it is clear that we can overcome every evil temper, every sin, and every temptation. Not by our own strength, but only through surrendering to the power of God, permitting Jesus to dwell in our hearts constantly. "I can do all things through Christ who strengthens me" (Philippians 4:13). Remember, "He is able to keep you from stumbling, and to present you faultless before the presence of His glory with exceeding joy" (Jude 24). If we do not have sufficient faith in Christ to believe that He can keep us from sinning, then we really don't have the faith that is needed to enter the kingdom of God. We never have to yield to temptation, for the power of God is stronger than that of the power of Satan. "Because He that is in you is greater than he who is in the world" (1 John 4:4). Therefore, "the Lord knows how to deliver the godly out of temptations" (2 Peter 2:9). With so many promises from God let us not make excuses for sin, but place our trembling hand of faith in the hand of Jesus and receive divine strength.

I learned that when temptation comes we are to resist immediately and not focus on the temptation. "Submit to God, resist the devil and he will flee from you. Draw near to God and He will draw near to you" (James 4:7, 8). This can be done by trusting God (See Proverbs 3:5-7); Invite Jesus to live out His life in you through the Holy Spirit (See Luke 11:13; John 14:21); Hiding His word in our heart that we would not sin against Him (See Psalms 119:11); Focus on pure and holy things (Philippians 4:8); cultivate a habit of constant communion with God (1 Thessalonians 5:17); and the study of His Word (2 Timothy 2:15).

Keep in mind this promise: "God is faithful, who will not allow you to be tempted beyond what you are able, but with the temptation will also make the way of escape, that you may be able to bear it" (1 Corinthians 10:13). After I had read this verse over several times, remembering a comment made by another Christian and reflecting upon some of my experiences my heart was warmed with joy. I could be sure that our heavenly Father measures and weighs every trial before He permits it to come upon us. Out of His great love, He takes in consideration our knowledge of Him through our past experience and through His Word. He considers the circumstances and the strength of the one who is to stand under the proving and test, and He never permits the temptations to be greater than the capacity of resistance. That is what 1 Corinthians 10:13 is promising. If the person is overpowered, this can never be charged to God. But the one tempted was not vigilant and prayerful and did not trust the provisions God had abundantly in store for him. Christ never fails us in our hour of combat. We must claim the promise and meet the foe in the name of the Lord.

How can we escape from succumbing to temptation and what do we need to receive that we may be able to resist it? Grace! We are counseled to "come boldly to the throne of grace, that we may obtain mercy and find grace to help in the time of need" (Hebrews 4:16). The grace here that God is offering to us is His character/the fruit of the Spirit. Love, being at the top of the list, which all the others flow from. This all became even clearer to me when reading the promise given in 2 Corinthians 12:9. "My grace is sufficient for you, for *My strength* is made perfect in weakness. Therefore, most gladly I will rather boast in my infirmities, that the *power of Christ* may rest upon me" (emphasis added). For when we are honest with God with regard to our sins, repenting and making a true confession, recognizing our need and complete dependence upon Him, then we may receive cleansing from our sin and the power of Christ may rest upon us, imparting grace in that area of our life to bring about a transformation. Truly without repentance and confession I would make the power of the Gospel of no effect in my life. There is more to the Gospel than just forgiveness, it is all about a new heart/new mind, new purposes, and new motives. It is a *changed life*.

In the book of Acts 5:31 it reveals to us that repentance is a gift from God. And with Jesus saying, "Without Me you can do nothing" John 15:5, I realized that I could not even repent without His aid. We have no power within ourselves to turn from or resist evil. It is just not there. Sure we might make some outward reforms that make it appear that we are good, but we can never change our heart. "Can the Ethiopian change his skin or the leopard his spots? Then may you also do good who are accustomed to do evil?" Jeremiah 13:23. "For who can bring a clean thing out of an unclean? Not one" Job 14:4. It is only through the gift of repentance and the reception of the Holy Spirit in our lives that we can turn from sin.

Christ's Example

When Christ revealed to Peter the time of trial and suffering that was just before Him, Peter replied, "Far be it from You, Lord; this shall not happen to You!" (Matthew 16:22), and the Savior commanded, "Get thee behind Me, Satan." (Matthew 16:23). Was Jesus calling Peter Satan? No! Not at all. Satan was speaking through Peter, making him act the part of the tempter. Satan's presence was unsuspected by Peter, but Christ could detect the presence of the deceiver, and in His rebuke to Peter, he addressed the real foe and brought to Peter's attention whom he was listing to. It is no different today, as Satan works through people and they know it not. I have come to realize that *humanity is not our enemy*, but Satan is, and that many people have been seduced, overcome by the great deceiver and brought into slavery to him (See 2 Peter 2:19.) The enemy of our soul is ever seeking to cast a stumbling block before us in how we respond to people, so that we bring dishonor to Christ and wound him afresh making our profession of no effect. Remember we "wrestle not against flesh and blood, but against principalities, against powers, against the rulers of the darkness of this world, against spiritual wickedness in high places (Ephesians 6:12).

On one occasion, speaking to the twelve, and referring to Judas, Christ declared, "Did I not choose you, the twelve, and one of you is a devil?" (John 6:70) Did Jesus choose Satan to be His disciple? Of course not. However, often in the days of His earthly ministry the Savior met His adversary in human form, when Satan as an unclean spirit took possession of men. Yet Jesus, knowing that Judas would betray Him, still washed his feet. (See John 13:12.) When Judas betrayed Him with a kiss, Jesus looked upon him with sympathy and with love in His voice said, *"Friend,* why have you come?" (See Matthew 26:47-50, emphasis supplied) Jesus knew all through His ministry that Judas was being seduced by Satan, yet Jesus drew near to him seeking to awaken his mind to another Master that could set him free from sin. Also when Jesus was being crucified He prayed for His enemies with a request: "Father, forgive them, for they do not know what they do" (Luke 23:34). In these stories and more, it became clear to me that as a Christian I am to *love the sinner but hate the sin.* Jesus was ever seeking to draw humanity to God the Father through love and compassion, always responding to a negative situation in a positive way. Truly, He is our example.

The Gospels tell us of His life, His battle with Satan in the wilderness, and His example to us in the power of the Word. Throughout His life he ministered to the people, encouraging them, praying for them, and lovingly pleading with the sinner to turn from evil. Read His beautiful prayer on behalf of His disciples and all those that would believe in Him through their testimony (John 17).

In the closing scenes of the Gospel we can behold Him lying on the ground in the garden of Gethsemane, praying to His Father, "O, My Father, if this cup may not pass away from me except I drink it, Thy will be done." Three times He uttered that prayer. Three times His humanity caused Him to shrink from the last, crowning sacrifice. However, I believe it was at this point that the history of the human race came up before Him. He could see that the transgressors of the law, if left to ourselves, would perish. He could see our helplessness and the power of sin, the woes and lamentations of a doomed world. He could behold our impending fate, and so His decision was made. He chose to save you and me, my friend, at the cost of Himself. He accepted His baptism of blood that through His sacrifice the perishing millions could gain everlasting life. He would not turn from His mission. He became the Savior of a race that has willed to sin. As He wrestled with that inner self not to do His own will, He was strengthened. His prayer became only submission: "If this cup may not pass away from Me, except I drink it, Thy will be done" (Matthew 26:36-42; Mark 14:32-39; Luke 22:39-46). Here again, Christ showed us the way to victory though submission to the will of God, and in return He received the strength He needed to carry out His mission. Here we are encouraged to "look unto Jesus, the author and finisher of our faith, who for the joy that was set before Him endured the cross, despising the shame, and has sat down at the right hand of the throne of God" (Hebrews 12:2).

Note how He expresses His love for Judas, who had betrayed Him, by addressing him *"friend,* why have you come?" (Matthew 26:50 emphasis mine). Note how He treated one that treated Him as an enemy, by healing an ear that had been cut off (Luke 22:49-51). Read in the closing scenes of the Gospels how the spiritual leaders of His day falsely accused, condemned, spat on, ridiculed, and mocked Him. Read how the Roman judge pronounced Him faultless but then scourged Him and handed Him over to be crucified. Yet, even while hanging on the cross, He prayed for His enemies (Luke 23:34), and forgave and encouraged a thief hanging next to Him (Luke 23:42, 43). "He was wounded for our transgressions. He was bruised for iniquities (sins); the chastisement for our peace was upon Him, and by His stripes we are healed" (See Isaiah 53:5.) As He experienced total separation from His Father we read of His bitter cry, "My God, My God, why hast thou forsaken Me?" (Matthew 27:46). He then yielded up His spirit. *Behold, my friend, the Lamb of God who died for you and me!* So I ask you my friend, now, will you trust Him?

I invite you to behold your Creator, Jesus Christ (Colossians 1:16), who has left the courts of heaven, where all is purity, happiness, and glory, to save the one lost sheep, the one world that has fallen to sin. He had the form of God and was equal to Him, but he took the form of a bondservant (slave) and came to us in the likeness of man … the seed of Abraham and experienced the sufferings of temptation so He would be able to comfort us that are being tempted (See Philippians 2:6, 7; Hebrews 2:16 -18.)

However, praise God it did not end there on the cross. Today we serve a risen Savior, who stands at the right hand of God as High Priest and Mediator. Jesus has made it possible for us to come to that throne of grace to receive strength in our time of need. He is knocking at the door of your heart, will you let Him in? (See 1Timothy 2:5; Hebrews 4:15, 16; Revelation 3:20.)

Notations

One of the amazing things I found about the poem in chapter 7, page 34 was how many Bible scriptures are related to it. I encourage you to go back and read it and then look up the following scriptures;

Jesus promised that He would never leave us or forsake us, and that He would be with us unto the end of the world (Hebrews 13:5 and Matthew 28:20). I have learned that He is touched with our infirmities (Hebrews 4:15). He invites us to bring our burdens to Him, for He cares for us and wants us to learn from His example (See Matthew 11:28-30; Hebrews 4:16; 1 Peter 5:7; Psalms 46:1 55:22.)

All things are possible with God (Luke 1:37). His Word also tells us that God has given everyone a measure of faith, and that Jesus is the Author and Finisher of our faith (See Romans 12:3 Hebrews 12:2.)

Jesus tells us the signs of the end, and as we look at what is happening in our day and what the Scriptures say, it becomes clear that the time of His return is soon (See Matthew 24; Luke 21:8-11, 25-28; 2 Timothy 3:1-5.)

He also tells us that our faith will be tested (See James 1:12; 1 Peter 1:7; 4:12.) That His Spirit will reach us wherever we are (See Psalms 139:7-10.) We are to trust in the Father and Son for guidance and protection (See 2 Peter 1:19-21; 2 Timothy 3:16; Proverbs 3:5, 6; Psalms 37:39, 40, 46:1, 125:1.)

And we are called to love our neighbors and our enemies as Christ loved us (See Matthew 5:44-48, 22:39; Luke 6:27-38; John 13:34; 15:12, 17.) It is apparent that this world would be better if we loved God supremely, and one another as God loves us, for love is the fulfilling of the law (See Romans 13:10.)

After discovering these Bible verses, I have no doubt in my mind that God sent an angel that night, to reach me where I was. It sparked an interest to search for Him in His Word. To seek to know the God who demonstrated to me so much of His mercy and love.

The following is a list of key symbols and their meanings in Bible prophecy. Each symbol is in bold type and is followed by its corresponding literal meaning.

Angel = *Messenger*
Daniel 8:16; 9:21; Like 1:19, 26; Hebrews 1:14

Babylon = *Religious apostasy/confusion*
Genesis 10:8-10; 11:6-9; Revelation 18:2, 3; 17:1-5

Beast = *Kingdom/government/political power*
Daniel 7:17, 23

Bread = *Word of God*
John 6:35, 51, 52, 63

Day = *Literal year*
Ezekiel 4:6; Numbers 14:34

Dragon = *Satan or his agency*
Isaiah 27:1, 30:6; Psalm 74:13, 14; Revelation 12:7-9 Ezekiel 29:3;
Jeremiah 51:34

Forehead = *Mind*
Romans 7:25; Ezekiel 3:8, 9

Hand = *Work*
Ecclesiastes 9:10

Harlot = *Apostate church/religion*
Isaiah 1:21-27; Jeremiah 3:1-3, 6-9

Heads = *Major powers/ rulers/governments*
Revelation 17:3, 9, 10

Horn = *King or kingdom*
Daniel 7:24; 8:5, 21, 22; Zechariah 1:18, 19; Revelation 17:12

Lamb = *Jesus/sacrifice*
John 1:29; 1 Corinthians 5:7

Lamp = *Word of God*
Psalm 119:105

Lion = *Jesus Christ*
Revelation 5:4-9

Mark = *Sign or seal of approval or disapproval*
Ezekiel 9:4; Romans 4:11; Revelation 13:17; 14:9-11; 7:2, 3

Mountains = *Political or religio-political powers*
Isaiah 2:2, 3; Jeremiah 17; 3; 31:23; 51:24, 25; Ezekiel 17:22, 23;
Daniel 2:35, 44, And 45

Oil = *Holy Spirit*
Zechariah 4:2-6; Revelation 4:5

Red = *Sin/corruption*
Isaiah 1:18; Nahum 2:3;
Revelation 17:1-4

Rock = *Jesus /truth*
1 Corinthians 10:4; Isaiah 8:13, 14; Romans 9:33; Matthew 7:24

Seal = *Sign or mark of approval or disapproval*
Romans 4:11; Revelation 7:2, 3

Serpent = *Satan*
Revelation 12:9; 20:2

Stars = *Angels/messengers*
Revelation 1:16, 20; 12:4, 7-9; Job 38:7

Sun = *Jesus/the gospel*
Psalm 84:11; Malachi 4:2; Matthew 17:2; John 8:12; 9:5

Sword = *Word of God*
Ephesians 6:17; Hebrews 4:12

Thief = *Suddenness of Jesus' coming*
1 Thessalonians 5:2-4; 2 Peter 3:10

Time = *Literal year*
Daniel 4:16, 23, 25, 32; 7:25; Daniel 11:13 margin

Waters = *Inhabited area/ people, nations*
Revelation 17:15

White Robes = *Victory/ righteousness*
Revelation 19:8; 3:5; 7:14

Winds = *Strife/commotion/"winds of war"*
Jeremiah 25:31-33; 49:36, 37; 4:11-13; Zechariah 7:14

Woman, Pure = *True church*
Jeremiah 6:2; 2 Corinthians 11:2; Ephesians 5:23-27

Woman, Corrupt = *Apostate church*
Ezekiel 16:15-58; 23:2-21; Hosea 2:5; 3:1; Revelation 14:4

You can sign up for your free Bible studies at Amazing Facts at P.O. Box 909, Roseville, CA 95678-0909, or go to www.amazingfacts. org and receive information on several topics. I hope you receive a greater knowledge of God from these studies. I know that I sure have. May God richly bless you as you study and share the Good News with others!

For more information about *Christmas Behind Bars* please go to www.christmasbehindbars.com

For more information on gardening - Go to YouTube and type in *"Back to Eden by Paul Gautschi"*

For more information on genetic engineering GMO- Go to YouTube and type in *"The world according to Monsanto"* (full length documentary). Also check out another documentary entitled – *"Genetic Roulette - the gamble of our lives."*

About the Author

I am currently working for myself doing construction work. My wife and I have been traveling over the years speaking at churches, schools, and prisons. We enjoy speaking to all denominations, sharing the power of God's grace in word and songs. We also enjoy helping our good friend, Lemuel Vega, with a prison ministry program called *Christmas Behind Bars.* We look forward to being used by God as tools in His hands to win souls for Jesus Christ. It is our prayer that His will be done in our lives.

If you would like to invite us to speak at your local church, school, prison, small group or camp meeting, or you want to make a donation, you may contact us at:

ministryoftruth7@gmail.com

Or call 1-574-532-2119